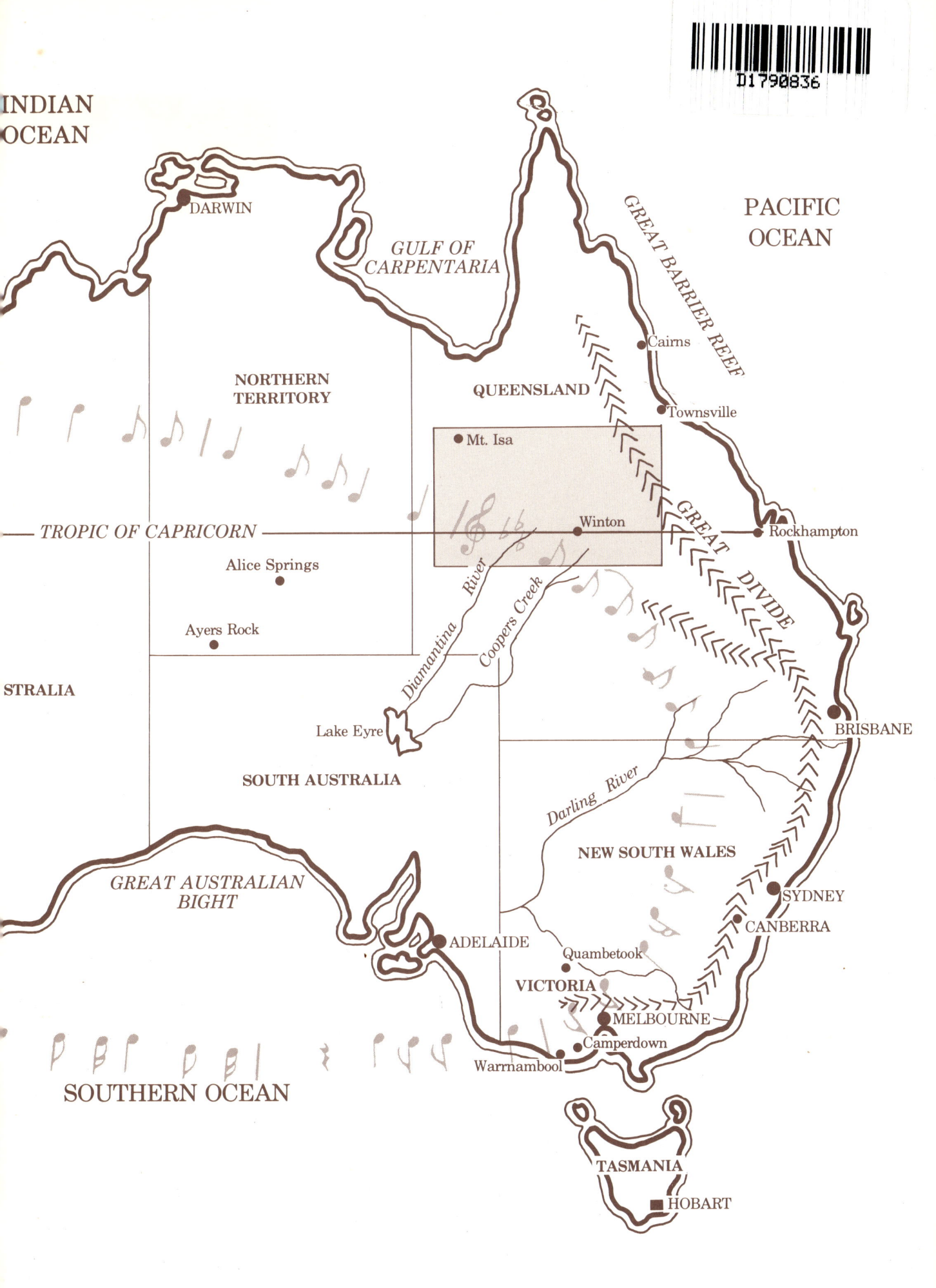

"WALTZING MATILDA"
SONG OF AUSTRALIA

"WALTZING MATILDA"
SONG OF AUSTRALIA
A folk-history by
·RICHARD MAGOFFIN·

MIMOSA PRESS PUBLISHERS
Charters Towers
North Queensland 4820

© Richard Magoffin 1983
All rights reserved

First published by Mimosa Press, Publishers, Australia, 1983.

National Library of Australia
Cataloguing-in-publication data:

Magoffin, Richard,
Waltzing Matilda — Song of Australia
ISBN 0 9598986 4 6

Typesetting and colour separation,
Hong Kong
Printed in Hong Kong

Acknowledgements

Individuals:
Rev. Fr. Vernon Allen, Dr. Colin Roderick, Dr. Clement Semmler, Dr. Russell Ward. Messrs Chas T. Alexander, W.H. Anning, Fred Archer, J.R.Y. Bartlam, W.R.F. Bolton, Kevin Brosnan, Harold De Boos, Robert Curr, Viv Desailly, W.N. ('Pug') Douglas, Peter Evert, Vince Evert, Jim Francis, Mick Griffin, Jack Huey, H. Lamb, Henry Lamond, John Manifold, Sydney May, Frederick T. Macartney, Dave Milne, George Morrison, Dan Nicholson, Hugh Paterson, Dagworth Pene, William Power, Alan Queale, Malcolm Rea, Tom Shanahan, Ron Sharman, Bruce Simpson, Arthur Stirling, Walter Stone, Andrew Taylor, Gilbert Weale.

Rev. Mother Keiran, Mesdames Violet Allingham, Helen Anderson, Effie Berryman, Kitty Carter, Carol Curr, Eileen Dooner, Cecily Douglas, Dorothy Gibson-Wilde, Eileen Heard, Beatie Landsberg, Islay McIntosh, Barbara Roulston, Dorothy Witney. Misses Leslie Macpherson, Barbara May, and Melissa Jones.

Intsitutions and companies:
The Australian Broadcasting Commission, The Australian National University Library, Allans Music (Aust) Pty. Ltd., Angus and Robertson Pty. Ltd., The British Museum, The Central Library, Rochester, Kent, Cloncurry Shire Council, Cobb and Co., The Corporation of Paisley, Scotland, Dublin Public Library, The English Folk Song and Dance Society, Lansdowne Press, The Latrobe Library, Lionel Lindsay Museum and Art Gallery, The Mitchell Library, The National Library of Scotland, Postmaster General's Department, Queensland Education Department, Queensland Police Department, Queensland State Archives, Registrar General, Brisbane, The Royal College of Organists, W. R. Smith and Paterson, Tasmanian State Library, Warrnambool Racing Club, Winton Historical Society, Winton Shire Council, Winton Tourist Promotion Association, The Australian Photographic Agency, Melbourne.

Bibliography
Australia's Music, Roger Covell.
Winton Jubilee Book, Father Burke.
The Worker's First Seventy Years, The Worker Newspaper.
Reminiscences of Queensland, W.H. Corfield.
Cobbers, Thomas Wood.
Folksongs of Australia, Meredith and Anderson.
Old Bush Songs, A.B. Paterson,
Saltbush Bill J.P. and other verses, A.B. Paterson.
Three Elephant Power, A.B. Paterson.
Australia for the Australians, A.B. Paterson.
The Collected Verse of A.B. Paterson.
The Banjo of the Bush, Clement Semmler.
Henry Lawson — the Grey Dreamer, Denton Prout.
The Works of Henry Lawson.
Who Wrote the Ballads, John Manifold.
The Story of Waltzing Matilda, Sydney May (Two Editions).
On the origins of Waltzing Matilda, Harry Pearce.
A Waltz with Matilda, Oscar Mendelsohn.
Pro Hart's Waltzing Matilda, Graham Jenkin.

Newspapers and periodicals
Meanjin, Australian Signpost, A.B.C. Weekly, The Camperdown Chronicle, The Warrnambool Standard, The Northern Miner, The North Queensland Register, The Queenslander, The Brisbane Courier, The Courier Mail, The Sunday Mail, The Sydney Morning Herald, The Age, The Yale Review, Yass Tribune Courier, Walkabout, The Australian, The Longreach Leader, People, The Bulletin, National Folk.

Photo credits
The Australian Picture Library, Sydney.
Tony Dell Productions, Brisbane.
The Australian Photographic Agency, Melbourne.
Peter C. Ford, Brisbane.
Bay Books, Sydney.
Queensland Government Tourist Bureau
Queensland Newspapers, Brisbane.

Contents

Foreword	7
Preface	9
The Swag and a Kangaroo	11
The Poet	17
The Music	26
The Pianist	28
The Boiling Billy	34
The Jumbuck	42
The Swagman and Policemen	47
The Squatter	50
The Billabong	59
The Song	63
The Manuscript	67
The Towns and Cities	71
The World	78
The Ghost	82
Appendix	90

Also by Richard Magoffin:
WE BUSHIES
CHOPS AND GRAVY
FAIR DINKUM MATILDA
DOWN ANOTHER TRACK

Dedication

This book is dedicated to the memory of the unsung pioneers of North Western Queensland, squatters and bagmen alike, who helped forge the Australian ideal of a "fair go" for everyone.

Foreword

PRIME MINISTER

CANBERRA

31st May, 1983

It gives me great pleasure to be associated with this book by Richard Magoffin, an Australian who has done so much to lay to rest the ghost of Matilda. From the time it was written in 1895 at Dagworth Station to the present time, *Waltzing Matilda* has been a song of remarkable national popularity and, of course, has even been considered as a contender for our national anthem.

There is a certain irony in this, my contribution, from Canberra. Banjo Paterson spent two important phases of his life in this area, periods in which his love of the bush, conceptions of country life, love of adventure and appreciation of humour were developed and nurtured and later reinforced after periods of city living. His boyhood years at Illalong Station near Yass had a profound effect on his impressions of country life and country people and it was during these years that he developed his lasting love of horses and racing. After many years of city living, and now in his 40's, he returned to the bush and settled at Coodra Vale Station on the river flats of the Goodradigbee River near Wee Jasper. With typical Paterson humour he is said to have been delighted with his new home because it made his trips south for the Melbourne Cup much shorter.

Paterson's poetry is widely regarded as having built the Australian bushman and his lifestyle into a legend. *Waltzing Matilda* is no exception. *Waltzing Matilda*, and other Paterson poetry, has caught the spirit of a period in Australia's development and through its simple and readily-identifiable images, ensured that future generations of Australians have an understanding and appreciation of Australian life as it once was.

Richard Magoffin has assisted this process by providing this history of *Waltzing Matilda* and the people and times in which it was written. Any attempt to make this, Australia's best known song, better understood and appreciated, is to be congratulated.

WALTZING MATILDA

Oh! there once was a swagman camped in the Billabong
    Under the shade of a Coolabah tree,
And he sang as he looked at his old billy boiling
    'Who'll come a-waltzing Matilda with me?'

Who'll come a-waltzing Matilda my darling,
    Who'll come a-waltzing Matilda with me?
Waltzing Matilda and leading a waterbag
    Who'll come a-waltzing Matilda with me?

Down came a jumbuck to drink at the water-hole,
    Up jumped the swagman and grabbed him in glee;
And he sang as he put him away in his tuckerbag,
    'You'll come a-waltzing Matilda with me.'

Down came the squatter a-riding his thoroughbred;
    Down came policemen — one, two, three.
'Whose is the jumbuck you've got in the tuckerbag?
    You'll come a-waltzing Matilda with me.'

But the swagman, he up and he jumped in the water-hole,
    Drowning himself by the Coolabah tree,
And his ghost may be heard as it sings in the Billabong,
    'Who'll come a-waltzing Matilda with me?'

                                A. B. Paterson.
               Reproduced from 'Saltbush Bill J. P. and
                    Other Verses', published 1917.

Preface

Over seventy years ago, in his book, *The Dreadnought of the Darling*, C. E. W. Bean, that great social historian of peace and of war, wrote:

The Australian, one hundred to two hundred years hence, will still live with the consciousness that, if he only goes far enough back, over the hills and across the plains, he comes to the end of the half desert country where men have to live the lives of strong men. And the life of that mysterious country will affect the Australian imagination much as the life of the sea has affected that of the English.

No truer words — about the Australian ethos, about the inspiration of much that is best in our art, music and literature — have been written.

It was this perception that inspired writers from Henry Lawson and Banjo Paterson to Xavier Herbert, Eleanor Dark, Frank Dalby Davison and those of our modern writers who still find in the magic of our great continent a never-failing challenge for their art.

No-one could be more conscious of this than Richard Magoffin, who has devoted his life to chronicling the ceaseless battle of the ordinary outback Australian, the bushie, with an environment at once hostile and yet in so many ways eventually rewarding.

In the preface to the second edition of my biography of A. B. Paterson, *The Banjo of the Bush*, I wrote of Magoffin as "Queenslander and 'bushie', bush balladist and scholar", referring especially to his splendidly documented and researched book, *Fair Dinkum Matilda*, in which he laid for ever the ghost of any doubt about the writing of our truly national song by Paterson.

I wrote, inter alia, that Richard Magoffin had earned "his particular place in our literary history." Just to prove that I was right, here he is again with a fascinating folk history of Matilda; a guided tour, if you like, down all the highways and byways of the one Australian song that has reached the hearts of people in almost every corner of the world.

He has fossicked out veritable gems of discovery that reflect the multitudinous facets of Paterson's song — not only its words and music — but also the lives and destinies of those who impinged, in greater or lesser way, on the making of the song.

Richard Magoffin, a dedicated North Queensland countryman, is, in many ways, the very epitome of the Australian character forged in the literature of the Golden Age of the 1890s. To a love of the outback he has added zeal and enthusiasm to keep alive its traditions and continually to remind his urban brothers of them, lest they forget the eternal truths of our great continent.

Clement Semmler

Dr Clement Semmler

The Swag and a Kangaroo

Who was Matilda?

Since the Twelfth Commonwealth Games at Brisbane, in 1982, many people overseas and in this country could be excused for believing Matilda to be a giant kangaroo with huge eyes and a captivating wink.

The Matilda who has been immortalised in Australia's national song was not a native of the land like the kangaroo. Like many of our forebears, she came from Europe seeking gold, found little and, with little choice, decided to make her way in this country, adopting the land and its people as her own.

In making that one-way journey, Matilda followed an age-old precedent and it is only in recent times that Australians in any number have been able to cross the wide oceans to visit the lands of their ancestors.

Our first settlers walked here from the North thousands of years ago and adopted a nomadic life which allowed them to wander as far South as Tasmania. Then the ice melted and their land bridges were cut. They remained isolated from the rest of the world, except for several invasions and occasional visits by Asian fishermen and European navigators, until 26th January, 1788.

In 1783, following the American Revolution of 1776, Britain, having lost her dumping ground for unwanted persons, decided on a new and even more distant repository for felons then overcrowding her gaols and river hulks. On 23rd January, 1787, it was announced in Parliament that Lord Sydney agreed to transport convicts to New South Wales.

Under the command of Captain Arthur Phillip, 1,400 persons, including 780 convicts, sailed from Portsmouth on 13th May in eleven ships: *H.M.S. Sirius*, Flagship, *Borrowdale*, *Alexander*, *Scarborough*, *Charlotte*, *Fishburn*, *Golden Grove*, *Prince of Wales*, *Lady Penrhyn*, *Friendship*, and *H.M.S. Supply*.

After eight months and fifteen thousand miles, the lead ships reached Botany Bay. Deciding that this area was unsuitable, Captain Phillip soon settled on Port Jackson, nine miles to the North. Here, at a quiet little cove with a freshwater stream, he landed with his miserable human cargo and their guards on 26th January, 1788, to establish the penal settlement of Sydney and so set the cornerstone upon which was built the Australian nation — and her character.

It is all too easily forgotten today that Australia was founded by convict slaves under a cruel colonial dictatorship — founded under the lash by slaves in chains — founded with human suffering, degradation, starvation, hopelessness and the despair of those who were forced under the ever-present threat of the gallows to quarry the stone, fell the forest and till the unwilling soil.

Australia was founded by felons with a living hatred for authority.

Matilda was not one of those first settlers; in fact, she was not to arrive for more than fifty years and then she came as a free settler. Nevertheless, today she reminds us with her travelling companion, a felon, a sheep-stealing swagman, that Australians will never tolerate the cruelty and injustices which our first settlers suffered. Above all else, *Waltzing Matilda* remains the *Ballad of the Fair Go*.

Somehow, the forlorn little colony at Sydney survived. Sufficient stores arrived to supplement the hard-won and meagre produce of the land. It was not until 1813 that three men, Lawson, Blaxland and Wentworth, were able to find a way over the Great Dividing Range through the Blue Mountains to the wide, fertile plains beyond. These plains would soon provide food, not only for the colony of New South Wales, but for much of the world.

Soon also, these plains would be home for thousands of people from all over the world — hordes of free settlers seeking gold. They followed Edward Hargraves who discovered alluvial gold near Bathurst in February, 1851. The find

Matilda, hostess of the Twelfth Commonwealth Games, Brisbane, 1982. A giant kangaroo with a captivating wink.

was announced in the *Sydney Morning Herald* on 15th May, 1851. There had been two small finds near Bathurst in 1823 and near Lithgow in 1839 and 1841, but what made Hargraves' discovery particularly newsworthy was that he had said previously that he would find gold where he did. While on the Californian diggings, he had noticed the similarity of geological formations there with others he had seen in Australia eighteen years previously. He took a ship back to Sydney, telling his travelling companions of the certainty that he would find gold. They laughed at him, as did those to whom he spoke in Sydney.

On 5th February, Hargraves set out alone on horseback to cross the Blue Mountains. On the 12th he found gold at his first attempts, just where he expected it to be.

Hargrave's discovery was followed soon afterwards in Victoria by W. Campbell's, at Clunes in June; by T. Hiscock's, near Ballarat in August; and by H. Frenchman's, at Bendigo in December. The Australian Gold Rush had begun.

In a few years, the population of the colonies was to double and this growth was accompanied by a great change in character. Unlike our first reluctant settlers, these newcomers crossed the great oceans bound for the new goldfields with hope, with ambitions and dreams, and with a willingness to work for themselves. They brought with them an independent spirit which colonial authorities would find difficult to handle. One eye-witness to the immediate social effects of the discovery of gold was G. C. Mundy. He wrote in *Our Antipodes* (London, 1855): *'Nothing, indeed, can have a more levelling effect upon society than the power of digging gold. It can be done, for a time at least, without any capital but that of health and strength; and the man inured to toil, however ignorant, is on more than equal terms with the educated and refined in a pursuit involving so much personal hardship.'*

One who came to the Victorian diggings in 1851 was the author's great-grandfather. He came to Ballarat from Northern Ireland.

From all over the world they came to find gold. They came from the British Isles, from Europe and Scandanavia, from Asia and from the Americas. A few were lucky, but most found little. Some left to seek their fortunes elsewhere, but most stayed to build a nation from what had been a penal colony founded on human misery. The new Australia and its society would be one

DIGGERS ON W

THE ROMANC

The Australian swag was born of Australia and no other land — of the great lone land of magnificent distances and bright heat; the land of self-reliance, and never-give-in, and help-your-mate. The grave of many of the world's tragedies and comedies — royal and otherwise. The land where a man out of employment might shoulder his swag in Adelaide and take the track, and years later walk into a hut on the Gulf, or never be heard of any more, or a body be found in the bush and buried by the mounted police, or never found and never buried — what does it matter?

The land I love above all others — not because it was kind to me, but because I was born on

Sketched on the spot.

O BENDIGO.

OF THE SWAG

Australian soil, and because of the foreign father who died at his work in the ranks of Australian pioneers, and because of many things, Australia! My country! Her very name is music to me. God bless Australia! for the sake of the great hearts of the heart of her! God keep her clear of the old-world shams and social lies and mockery, and callous commercialism, and sordid shame! And heaven send that, if ever in my time her sons are called upon to fight for her young life and honour, I die with the first rank of them and be buried in Australian ground.

Henry Lawson, 1901.

based on hope, on free aspirations, free enterprise and its wealth for those willing to work and a fair share for those who couldn't. The struggle for the achievement of these aspirations would be long and bitter, before colonial autocracy would give way to the establishment of one of the world's purest democracies.

With those who came in their thousands during the 1850s was Matilda. It is not known exactly when or with whom she came. Perhaps she came direct from Germany, Austria, Bavaria, or one of the other mid-European countries. Possibly, she came to the goldfields with German settlers who crossed into Victoria from South Australia *auf der walz Mathilde*.

Most Australians know that *Matilda* was the name given by swagmen to their blanket rolls or swags and that *waltzing Matilda* means *humping bluey, on the wallaby*, and *on the track*, but why Matilda? How did the swag acquire this name? Why not Polly or Amelia, Lily, or any other name? Why Matilda?

Those who have researched this question have soon found themselves looking into European history and folklore where so much of our Australian language has its roots. Soon too, we have found ourselves delving into the sordid past of a woman of ill-repute.

Mathilde was the name given by German soldiers to their camp followers during the *Thirty Years War* (1618-1643). It was further believed that the soldiers' greatcoats also came to be called *Mathilde* and that this nomenclature occurred through men having to lie all night in cold, wet trenches, wearing their coats, instead of being kept warm by real life Matildas in the flesh!

During the Middle Ages, a tradesman's pack used to be called *Mathilde* and one authority states that Austrian soldiers gave the name to the blanket roll which they carried. Furthermore, in the old days of the industrial guilds, the journeyman apprentice, carrying his pack from place to place, spoke of this as *going on the waltz*, while memoirs of early printers always referred to their probationary wanderings as *auf der walz*.

Young journeymen, as they travelled from mill to mill, would form liaisons with Mathildes or Metzes (another related nick-name) who would tramp the road with them, cooking, mending, and otherwise attending to their needs. It seems likely that the expression *walz Mathilde* was borrowed from the journeymen by the Austrian and German armies. Did these long dead soldiers once march to a bawdy *Waltzing Matilda*?

Matilda's tarnished ancestry can be traced even further — back to ancient Nordic mythology. There we find that a band of amazon type females were called *Hilde*, after an even earlier goddess of battle and warfare. Apparently, the esteemed name of *Hilde* degenerated over the centuries, possibly because of mixed militia — a worthwhile early experiment involving male and female warriors going into battle as one unit. Later, the term *mechild* evolved to describe the descendants of these amazons as camp followers. It is from this name that the word *metze* is derived and which is still in use today to describe a common prostitute.

It is possible that the term *Waltzing Matilda* entered the English language during the War of Spanish Succession. This long war, fought from 1701 to 1714, began when Charles II of Spain died without issue. The protagonists were Spain and France on one side, with England, Austria and the United Provinces, which included the Low Countries or Netherlands on the other. Austrian troops, allied to England, fought with the English soldiers under their general, the Duke of Marlborough. Well then, did Marlborough's men, marching and fighting beside Austrian soldiers in Holland and Spain, learn a bawdy *Walz Mathilde* from them?

Never mind — we know that Matilda was an earthy type and a loyal companion to the travelling worker in the early days in Europe. She apparently had little difficulty in assuming the same comforting role in Australia with our itinerant bush workers — the swagmen.

It seems fairly certain that Matilda migrated to Australia with those who came to search for gold and she was almost certainly present to see the rebel Southern Cross flag raised over the miners' stockade at Eureka on the Ballarat diggings.

The miners, 10,000 of them, had met on Bakery Hill, on Saturday, 11th November, 1854, to demand political reforms: full and fair representation, manhood suffrage, no property qualification of members for the Legislative Council, payment of members and short duration of Parliament. The immediate objects of the Ballarat Reform League were: change in management of the goldfields by disbanding the Commissioners, total abolition of diggers' and storekeepers' licence tax and a thorough and organised agitation of the goldfields and towns. The diggers saw the iniquitous Licence Fee as an unjust tax for people who had no representation.

The meeting on Bakery Hill carried a number of motions complaining of the lack of justice in the colony, of corrupt, dishonest, selfish and narrow-minded government and of tyranny with obnoxious laws and dishonest ministers. The meeting adopted the principles and objects of the Ballarat Reform League:

That it is the inalienable right of every citizen to have a voice in making the laws he is called upon to obey. That taxation without representation is tyranny.

That, being as the people have been hitherto, unrepresented in the Legislative Council of the Colony of Victoria, they have been tyrannized over, and it becomes their duty as well as interest to resist, and, if necessary to remove the irresponsible power which so tyrannized over them.

That this colony has hitherto been governed by paid officials, upon the false assumption that law is greater than justice, because, forsooth, it was made by them and their friends, and admirably suits their selfish ends and narrowminded views.

It is the object of the league to place the power in the hands of responsible representatives of the people to frame wholesome laws and carry on an honest Government.

That it is not the wish of the league to effect an immediate separation of this colony from the parent country, if equal laws and equal rights are dealt out to the whole free community; but that, if Queen Victoria continues to act upon the ill advice of dishonest ministers, and insists upon indirectly dictating obnoxious laws for the colony, under the assumed authority of the Royal prerogative, the Reform League will endeavour to supersede such Royal prerogative by asserting that of the people, which is the most royal of all prerogatives, as the people are the only legitimate source of all political power.

Refusal of the Colonial authorities to meet the diggers' demands led to further agitation, culminating in a mass meeting on 29th November, at which many of the diggers, following the exhortations of their leaders, burned their licences.

On the following day, an attempt was made by the authorities to arrest unlicensed miners. A riot ensued; the Riot Act was read; the military called in, and shots were exchanged, but without any loss of life.

'Matilda migrated with those who came to search for gold.'
The replica "Endeavour" rounding the Opera House on Bennelong Point, Sydney Harbour.

Now the rebels erected a stockade, consecrated and raised the Australian flag of independence, swearing vows to its defence. A resident Gold Commissioner, Mr Amos, was made prisoner and arraigned before the insurgent authorities.

The Colonial government reacted forcefully. The 99th Regiment having been brought over from Tasmania to defend Melbourne, the 12th and 40th Regiments were despatched to Ballarat. The military attacked with two field pieces and two howitzers early on the morning of 4th December.

Many of those who had manned the stockade were still away with their families. Some contemporary reports suggest that there were numerous desertions when it became known that an attack was imminent and it was obvious that the military commanders were well informed as to the situation in the stockade.

The battle was short and bloody. Thirty rebel diggers were killed and a large number wounded. A captain and three privates were killed, a lieutenant and eleven privates wounded.

The writer's great-grandfather was one of those who escaped the massacre as did the diggers' leader, Peter Lalor, who survived serious wounds to become a parliamentary representative.

Many of the rebels' demands for reform were subsequently met: the hated licence fee was replaced by a *Miners Right*, possession of which gave the right to vote in Electoral Districts established on the goldfields. The administration of the goldfields was changed. In June, 1855, Courts were established on the goldfields and wardens replaced the commissioners.

Peace descended upon the diggings and the Eureka flag was not to be seen flying again for another thirty-seven years. Then it was raised by revolutionary Union shearers in Central Western Queensland, in 1891, over the camps in which their forces were drilling in preparation for the seizure of the Central West. Again the rebels were put down with formidable force by the government of the day. It is today a little known fact that, had the rebels succeeded in their campaign, Australia would have seen the establishment of the world's first communist republic here instead of in Russia.

Matilda saw it all from the shoulders of the swagmen-shearers and it was from the ethos of these troubled times that she rose from her sordid past to become a woman of world renown. The instruments of her salvation and world acclaim were the poet, Andrew Barton Paterson and the pianist, Christina Macpherson.

The Poet

The Banjo, as he was affectionately known by Australians, was born Andrew Barton Paterson on 17th February, 1864, at Narambla, near Orange. He was the eldest of a family of two sons and five daughters. His father, Andrew Bogle Paterson, came of an old Scottish family and his mother was Rose, daughter of Robert Johnstone Barton.

There is evidence to support the belief that poets are born, not made, for Banjo's father preceded him as a contributor of verse to The Bulletin, and afterwards a sister, Jessie, also had verses published in its columns. During schooldays in Sydney, Paterson lived happily with his grandmother, Mrs Robert Barton, who also wrote verse.

At the age of sixteen, his father having lost his property, Illalong, Banjo matriculated and was articled to a firm of solicitors. After being enrolled as a solicitor, he became managing clerk for another law firm, and later practised in the partnership, Street and Paterson.

When Clancy of the Overflow by the Banjo appeared in the 1889 Christmas number of The Bulletin, Rolf Boldrewood lauded it as the best bush ballad since Gordon. Further verses over the same pen-name aroused a lot of interest, but many people did not know the Banjo's identity until October, 1895, when The Man from Snowy River and Other Verses was released. The book's instant success was described in the London Literary Yearbook as without parallel in colonial literary annals, having given its author a public wider than that of any other living writer except Kipling. The first edition sold out in a fortnight, ten thousand sold in the first year and sales eventually exceeded 100,000.

This of course was the golden era of Australian writing and the heyday of the bush ballad — long before the days when gramophone and wireless arrived on the entertainment scene. As the modern media improved and more books became available, people no longer needed to remember yarns and anecdotes in rhyme and metre. So the bush ballads and their reciters went into a long decline.

Frederick Macartney wrote in his Introduction to Paterson's Collected Verse:

He writes as bush folk themselves would if they were able, and it is this that has made his poetry popular with them, and with city people to whom it is on that account just as interesting. It is not likely to be less so. Time, with the changes of a mechanical age, has already given a legendary attraction to some of the bush ways. When the future looks back to the past as we look to the middle ages, Paterson's poetry will probably have the aura of old minstrelsy. He best of all has sung the actions of bush life in that natural music of rhythm and rhyme, which has a perpetual general appeal.

The belief has grown in recent years that Paterson was the spokesman for the upper classes — for the Squattocracy — while Henry Lawson spoke for the workers and the underdogs.

In fact, Paterson's first published work was a political pamphlet entitled Australia for the Australians which he produced in 1888. He slated the existing land laws and decried the uneven distribution of the country's natural wealth.

Having worked as a law clerk and handled the work of several banks, he recognized the plight of the smaller property-holders. He hated the task of having to screw money out of people who didn't have it.

He studied history and economics and decided to put the world right. In Australia for the Australians he says:

To advance Australia we must advance the Australians and the question of individual advancement is really the question of the greatest national importance.

It may be said that we are already the most prosperous country in the world. It ought to be possible in a new country like this for every man with a willing pair of hands to be always employed, and at good wages. There should be

'And he sees the vision splendid
of the sunlit plains extended.'

Today's 'Clancy of the Overflow'.

constant openings for our young men with brains and ability to make good incomes. Poverty and enforced idleness of willing men should be unknown. Yet we find the working men constantly seeking employment in vain. There seem to be less and less openings or chances for the young men who are coming forward. In all the colonies an absurd proportion of the population is crowding into the towns. The professions are overcrowded.

Paterson recommended land reforms as a remedy for the prevalent unemployment and the drift to the cities:

To anyone who understands the system of production, the way in which our inhabitants are crowding into the towns is something appalling: We would call a man a fool who ran a station with one-third of his hands at bookkeeping. We would think a mine pretty well doomed where the overseers and clerical hands numbered nearly as many as the working miners; and yet we have about one-third of our population in Sydney and suburbs alone! They are crowding into the townships, cutting one another's throats to get employment, most of them half their time idle. Why is this? The towns can only live on the produce of the country. They don't grow anything in the towns. If there is a bad season in the country it means so much the less to produce, so much the less to export, so much the less to employ town labour on. To whom does the finest house about Sydney belong? It belongs to a man who inherited a large fortune, made solely out of the rise and rents of real estate near Sydney; a man who counts his fortune by hundreds of thousands, and spends most of his time in England. He never did a day's work in his life, and yet can have every luxury, while thousands of his fellow country men have to toil and pinch and contrive to get a living. The more the country goes ahead the more he prospers, and the less he need do. It looks rather as if he 'had the loan of us' as the unrefined say. Yet it is not fair to blame the man. We should blame the rotten absurd system which makes such a thing possible.

Is this the writing of a capitalist, a spokesman for the upper classes?

The false classification of Paterson's work almost certainly sprang from the namecalling match in which he and Lawson engaged in 1892. Lawson called Banjo *a city bushman* and Banjo retaliated by calling Henry *a poet of the tomb.* Latterday critics have adopted Lawson's opinions of Paterson's work given during this rhyming match, quite forgetting that the whole thing was staged, it being a happy conspiracy between the two to inveigle a few extra pounds from Mr Archibald of *The Bulletin.*

That Paterson and Lawson held different views on politics and on the merits of bush and town, and that their personal circumstances and philosophies, and their approach to life and letters were at variance, is undeniable. It is equally undeniable that there was rivalry between them in their efforts to outdo each other as the best-selling Australian writer of the day. But that there was any real bitterness between them is untrue. It is interesting that Paterson felt they were both seeking the same 'reef'.

The two were really good friends, though it is easy to understand how the casual observer would be misled when 'Banjo wrote:

You had better stick to Sydney and make merry with the 'push',
For the bush will never suit you and you'll never suit the bush.

Henry retorted:

But you'll find it very jolly with the cuff and collar push,
And the city seems to suit you, while you rave about the bush.

Probably the false opinions of Paterson's attitude sprang directly from lines from Lawson such as these:

Would you like to change with Clancy — go a-droving? tell us true,
For we rather think that Clancy would be glad to change with you.

and

Do you think the bush was better in the 'good old droving days',
When the squatter ruled supremely as the king of western ways?

Some observers have said that Paterson saw life in style as though from a galloping horse, while Lawson saw it on foot. While there may be some grounds for this description, it probably pertains more to the actual works of the two, rather than to their motivations and sympathies.

Here again the genesis of this portrayal of Paterson can be seen in Lawson's lines:

It was pleasant up the country, City Bushman, where you went,
For you sought the greener patches and you travelled like a gent.

'Would you like to change with Clancy — go a-droving? — tell us true.'

Paterson was born into the squatting class while Lawson was born to battling parents in a bush tent. So naturally they would see things from different attitudes or altitudes. At the same time, although he moved in the upper circles of society, Paterson was a bushman at heart. He left an estate of only £230 when he died.

Lawson was being quite unfair in saying:
> It is up in Northern Queensland that the seasons do their best,
> But it's doubtful if you ever saw a season in the West.

Here Henry was on rather shaky ground. When he called Banjo a city bushman, it was really a case of the pot calling the kettle black. His experience of the outback was limited to a six months sojourn, mainly around Bourke, from September 1892 — after the rhyming match with Paterson.

I see an understanding tinged with envy and regret, in Lawson's feeling for Paterson's work in his concluding lines of 'City Bushman'.

> ....at times we long to gallop, where the reckless bushman rides,
> In the wake of startled brumbies that are flying for their hides,
> Long to feel the saddles tremble once again between our knees
> And to hear the stockwhips rattle just like rifles in the trees,
> Long to feel the bridle-leather tugging strongly in the hand,
> Long to feel once more a little like a native of the land!
> And the ring of bitter feeling in the jingling of our rhymes
> Isn't suited to the country or the spirit of the times.
> Let us go together droving, and returning, if we live,
> Try to understand each other while we reckon up the div.

They both did pretty well with their *divs*, and they did understand each other, as Paterson later

'It's up in Northern Queensland that the seasons do their best.'

revealed in his *Sydney Morning Herald* reminiscences:

We were working on space, and the pay was very small — in fact, I remember, I was paid exactly thirteen and sixpence for writing Clancy of the Overflow — so we slam-banged away at each other for weeks and weeks, not until they stopped us, but until we ran out of material. I think that Lawson put his case better than I did, but I had the better case, so that honours (or dishonours) were fairly equal. An undignified affair, but it was a case of 'root, hog or die'.

Denton Prout in *Henry Lawson — the Grey Dreamer* makes some good comments on Paterson. In referring to *The Man from Snowy River*, he says, *The author of this ballad Andrew Barton Paterson, then aged twenty-six, was in some respects a Jekyll-and-Hyde character. The son of a Scots pastoralist related to some of the best-known Sydney families, and with a public school and university background, Paterson was of an aloof and retiring disposition, strangely reticent regarding his opinions and emotions.*

Norman Lindsay once observed: *He was one of the most sardonically self-contained men I have ever met; he had more power to put you at a distance by one casual glance than any ostracism by words could do.*

Yet underneath the dour exterior Paterson presented to the world lurked a different personality, a devil-may-care, hail-fellow-well-met type of man, like a breezy young squatter on the spree. Victor Daley, the poet, was well aware of this hidden side of Paterson's personality, which was displayed only in his work:

Paterson has a sort of cavalier swagger and swing and suggestion of the hard-riding hero who killed three horses under him, and ate the third, being short of provisions, and slew several men upon the road and then drew up at an inn, gave the horse some whiskey in its corn, wiped the blood from his sword, kissed the maid of the inn, ordered a flagon of canary, drank it, and sat down to write a rollicking lyric.

'Long to feel the saddles tremble once again.'

'Beneath the sunshine and the stars.'

Few of Banjo's verses became songs. Waltzing Matilda is one of them, but, in this case, his words were written to an existing tune.

Another of his ballads which was widely sung in the bush also had something to say for the bush worker. This was *A Bushman's Song:*

> I asked a cove for shearin' once along the Marthaguy:
> 'We shear non-union here,' says he. 'I call it scab,' says I.
> I looked along the shearin' floor before I turned to go —
> There were eight or ten dashed Chinamen a-shearin' in a row.
> It was shift, boys, shift, for there wasn't the slightest doubt
> It was time to make a shift with the leprosy about.
> So I saddled up my horses, and I whistled to my dog,
> And I left his scabby station at the old jig-jog.
> I went to Illawarra, where my brother's got a farm:
> He has to ask his landlord's leave before he lifts his arm:
> The landlord owns the countryside — man, woman, dog, and cat,
> They haven't the cheek to dare to speak without they touch their hat.
> It was shift, boys, shift, for there wasn't the slightest doubt
> Their little landlord god and I would soon have fallen out;
> Was I to touch my hat to him? — was I his bloomin' dog?
> So I makes for up the country at the old jig-jog.
> But it's time that I was movin', I've a mighty way to go
> Till I drink artesian water from a thousand feet below;
> Till I meet the overlanders with the cattle comin' down —
> And I'll work a while till I make a pile, then have a spree in town.

Banjo himself covered a lot of country in his time and there is no doubt that, while he saw *the vision splendid of the sunlit plains extended and at night the wondrous glory of the everlasting stars,* he also saw the hardships of the bush worker, the squalor and the poverty in the cities.

Horsewomen of the West

Banjo was everyman's poet as the sales of his work have always shown. When he died in Sydney on 5th February, 1941, he left a nation-wide legacy which will live forever because many of his lines are as fresh today as they were when they came from his pen:

'Let us herd into the cities, let us crush and crowd and push
Till we lose the love of roving, and we learn to hate the bush;
And we'll turn our aspirations to a city life and beer,
And we'll slip across to England — it's a nicer place than here;
For there's not much risk of hardship where all comforts are in store,
And the theatres are in plenty, and the pubs are more and more.
But that ends it Mr Lawson, and it's time to say good-bye,
So we must agree to differ in all friendship, you and I.
Yes, we'll work our own salvation with the stoutest hearts we may,
And if fortune only favours we will take the road some day,
And go droving down the river 'neath the sunshine and the stars,
And then return to Sydney and vermilionize the bars.'

It was Banjo's custom in his spare time, to travel widely in the bush, though apparently fortune never favoured him to take the road on a droving trip with Lawson as he wished in those lines from 1892.

At that time the two young bards saw a lot of each other. In fact, Paterson was acting as Lawson's solicitor, particularly in regard to negotiations with Mr Archibald of the *Bulletin* and with Angus and Robertson who were later to publish Henry's work.

No doubt each influenced the other's writing and it is even possible that Lawson influenced Banjo's writing of *Waltzing Matilda*.

Late in 1894, Paterson again took to the bush, journeying through Western Queensland. At this time, he was collecting old bush ballads and songs wherever he went. Most of these were anonymous. They were eventually published by Angus and Robertson in 1905 in *Old Bush Songs* and it is significant that *Waltzing Matilda* was not included.

ON KILEY'S RUN

We lived the good old station life
On Kiley's Run,
With little thought of care of strife.
Old Kiley seldom used to roam,
He liked to make the Run his home;
The swagman never turned away
With empty hand at close of day
From Kiley's Run.

But droughts and losses came apace
To Kiley's Run,
Till ruin stared him in the face;
He toiled and toiled while lived the light,
He dreamed of overdrafts at night;
At length, because he could not pay,
His bankers took the stock away
From Kiley's Run.

The owner lives in England now
On Kiley's Run,
He knows a racehorse from a cow;
But that is all he knows of stock:
His chiefest care is how to dock
Expenses, and he sends from town
To cut the shearers' wages down
On Kiley's Run.

There runs a lane for thirty miles
Through Kiley's Run.
On either side the herbage smiles,
But wretched travelling sheep must pass
Without a drink or blade of grass
Through that long land of death and shame:
The weary drovers curse the name
Of Kiley's Run.

The name itself is changed of late
Of Kiley's Run.
They call it 'Chandos Park Estate'.
The lonely swagman through the dark
Must hump his swag past Chandos Park —
The name is English, don't you see:
The old name sweeter sounds to me
Of Kiley's Run.

I cannot guess what fate will bring
To Kiley's Run —
For chances come and changes ring —
I scarcely think 'twill always be
Locked up to suit an absentee;
And if he lets it out in farms
His tenants soon will carry arms
On Kiley's Run.

A.B. Paterson

'There runs a lane for thirty miles through Kiley's Run.'

The Music

'Thomas Bulch gave new life to band work in Australia.'

Just as our search for Matilda's ancestry took us to Europe, so, when we come to seek the origins of the tune which took Matilda from Australia to the world, again we find ourselves in the old countries.

Our song is identified all over the world today as distinctly Australian, yet we find that so many aspects of *Waltzing Matilda* are older than the nation itself. Like much of our culture and language, we have borrowed a lot in producing this song which is so essentially Australian.

Perhaps the words have been largely responsible for making *Waltzing Matilda* as Australian as Ayers Rock or the kangaroo, but, without that whimsical tune, there would have been no *jolly swagman*, no *jumbuck*, no *billy*, and no song.

The story of the music begins with the writing of an older ballad, *Thou Bonnie Wood O' Craigielea* by Robert Tannahill, of Paisley in Scotland. This poem first appeared in Tannahill's collection, *The Soldier's Return with Other Poems and Songs*, published in 1807.

The composer, James Barr, wrote music for the ballad, probably about 1805. The ballad with music was published in *The Miniature Museum of Scottish Songs and Music*, in 1818.

Tannahill was born in Castle Street, Paisley on 3rd June, 1774 and, ironically, committed suicide in the Scots equivalent of a billabong on 17th May, 1810.

The memory of the poet was kept green with annual concerts on his birthday when a choir of Paisley lads and lasses would render, unaccompanied, a selection of his songs.

The composer, James Barr (1781-1860) was born in Tarbolton but spent his early years in Kilbarchan. He emigrated to St John, New Brunswick in 1832, but later returned to Scotland and settled in Govan, Glasgow.

Another arrangement of the song was made by T.S. Gleadhill, but little is known of him other than that he edited *Kyle's Scottish Lyric Gems with Music*. (See appendix K)

There is a suggestion that the tune may originally have been set to an Irish air *Go to the Devil and Shake Yourself*, published in 1720. This air appears in several Irish and English collections under various titles. The City Librarian of Dublin Library, in a letter to the author, said that he thought he could detect a slight resemblance to *Waltzing Matilda*.

It would be nice to think that the Irish, as well as the Scots, English, Austrians and Germans, have played a part in providing Australia with her song. As we shall soon see, the Germans were to help with the music as well as the title.

Tannahill's ballad *Thou Bonnie Wood O' Craigielea* is still sung in Scottish schools to this day. While initially there may not appear to be any similarity to today's *Waltzing Matilda*, the reader needs to realise that there were several steps in the process through which our tune evolved. However, these steps can be eliminated to hear the melody ringing faintly through if the music of the old Scottish song is played in march tempo.

A march arrangement of the song was made in Australia during the early Nineties by Godfrey Parker. This was printed in Germany by Lyons and Company for their Band Journal and the first performance of this band item was at the Warrnambool Races, Victoria, on 24th April, 1894.

Craigielee by Godfrey Parker had earlier been printed in Thomas Bulch's *Colonial and Military Brass Band Journal*. Rare copies of the march are in existence, the author's having come from Arthur Stirling of Geelong, an authority on the history of Australian Brass Bands and their music.

Australia owes much to Thomas Bulch for the music of our national song, because he and Godfrey Parker were, in fact, one and the same person. Bulch's daughter, Mrs Johnson, of Geelong West, speaking of the pseudonyms used by her father, recalled that this was done as it was feared the public would tire of so many compositions from one person. Other names

H.R.H. the Duke of Edinburgh inspects the guard at the Twelfth Commonwealth Games.

employed by Bulch were: Henry Laski, Arthur Godfrey, and Eugene Lacosti, to name a few.

Thomas Edward Bulch was born on 30th December, 1860, at Shildon, Durhamshire, England. His father was a bandsman, as were three of his uncles, so, it was not surprising that, at the age of twelve, he joined a juvenile band formed by his uncle, Mr Dinsdale. Thomas composed his first contest march *The Typhoon* when he was seventeen.

In 1884, mainly for health reasons, Thomas Bulch migrated to Australia, bringing two of his bandsmen friends with him. They arrived in May of that year after a very rough voyage which Thomas never forgot. It was not long before *Bulch's Model Brass Band* was competing successfully at band contests in Victoria and New South Wales. This band eventually became the Ballarat City Band. So, the City of Ballarat enters our story a second time.

Bulch, with a partner, Mr Malthouse, conducted a music shop and warehouse in Sturt Street, Ballarat, and it was here that *Bulch's Brass Band Journal* was edited. Following a disastrous fire, which entirely burned out the premises, Bulch moved to Melbourne, where he conducted the Prahran Brass Band and the Melbourne Post Office Band.

Other moves were made to Sale and Albury and these two towns benefited greatly from his remarkable talent before he moved again, this time to Geelong. Here he spent some time, becoming a notable figure as he always wore a frock coat and bell topper, even when conducting. He wrote music for a living and had the ability to play piano with one hand and cornet with the other. Those who heard him said that it was a treat. His arrangement of *Craigielee* is said to have fitted his custom of making march arrangements of old Scottish songs.

When the First World War ended, Thomas Bulch accepted a position with Palings of Sydney. He then retired from bands, but had many private pupils whom he taught cornet, violin, and piano. He was still composing right up to the time of his last illness. One of his last compositions, *Bulch's Virtuoso Cornet School*, is held by Arthur Stirling in Geelong.

At seventy years of age and in indifferent health, the old musician could not combat his last illness and died at his home, 84 Ring Street, Mascot, Sydney, on 13th November, 1930.

The *Australian Band and Orchestral News* had this to say of Thomas Bulch:

> *His work will remain in the minds of those who knew him as a musician and a man. His coming to Australia gave new life to band work and thus passed a great benefactor to the musical world.*

The Pianist

The person deserving most credit for having given us the music of *Waltzing Matilda* was Christina Macpherson. It was she who played a tune to which Banjo Paterson wrote his words at Dagworth Station, North West Queensland, in January, 1895.

History introduces Christina much earlier. It was the crying of baby Christina which led to the downfall of Mad Dan Morgan, one of Australia's most notorious and most sadistic bushrangers.

Morgan chose not to be one of the order of 'gentlemen' bushrangers, for he was ruthless by nature and his moods were mercurial. His daring made him a legend. He spent a day at the races near Wagga Wagga, lunching in a booth with police officials, magistrates, and local dignitaries, later riding into the town itself.

During a coach hold-up, he made a squatter dance for his employees and a couple of swagmen, who were specially invited to the performance.

In June, 1864, with numerous crimes behind him, he shot a station-hand named Heriot during a drunken meal at Round Hill Station, Albury. Apologising immediately for his mistake, he sent another worker, John McLean, for a doctor. Then he shot McLean in the back and nursed him until he died.

The price on his head was now raised from £500 to £1,000, but Morgan continued to burn and shoot his way across the Riverina, apparently quite unworried, uncontrollable and quite contemptuous of the police.

While visiting Jerilderie, he jeered that the Victorian police would be no match for him, should he decide to cross the Murray River. A Victorian country newspaper accepted the challenge, declaring that, should he have the nerve to cross the river, he would be captured or dead within two days.

Partly for health reasons, as things were becoming a little too warm for him in New South Wales, the challenge and the climate appealed to Morgan.

In April, 1865, he crossed the Murray and gave notice of his arrival in Victoria by burning the haystack on the station of a former employer, threatening to shoot the owner, who fortunately was away. He then defiantly celebrated his second day south of the river by robbing McKinnon's station at Little River.

On the evening of Saturday, 8th April, Dan Morgan rode up to Pechelba, introduced himself, and ordered the MacPherson family into the homestead dining room.

The room was quite crowded for, apart from Mr and Mrs MacPherson, there were the two elder sons, Gideon and Jack and seven women, including Alice MacDonald, the nursemaid.

Feeling invigorated by more than the stipulated forty-eight hours in the fresh Victorian atmosphere, Morgan was in an affable mood. Passing pleasantries with the ladies, he requested supper and some music.

Having eaten well with good music, he became quite relaxed and drowsy. He was so confident that he allowed Alice MacDonald to go to the nursery in answer to the cries of the baby, Christina.

Alice slipped from the house and ran to Mr Rutherford's home nearby.

Rutherford arrived at the Wangaratta police station at 10.30 p.m. and soon afterwards, a detachment of forty troopers was headed for Pechelba.

Meanwhile, on her way back to the MacPherson home, Alice had passed the warning to a station hand, John Quinlan.

While Superintendent Cobham deployed his men around the house, instructing them to wait for daylight, Morgan's entertainment continued. He kept the family playing the piano and singing while he leisurely ate and drank the hours of his last night away.

At 8 o'clock in the morning, in drowsy good humour and accompanied by the MacPherson men, Morgan stepped carelessly from the front verandah into the station yard; 'Thank you for a

'Go back, go back, go back!'   **Galah**

delightful evening, gentlemen, and now, if you will accompany me to the yards and saddle your best horse for me, I'll be on my way.'

Totally oblivious to any danger and carrying a bridle in one hand, Morgan walked casually between the other men towards the stockyards.

> *Dawn broke upon the Murray, the morning mists were gone.*
> *The magpies sang their matins, the river murmured on.*
> *When Morgan left the homestead and neared the stockyard gate*
> *He heard the boobook's warning, and turned but turned too late*
> *For Quinlan pressed the trigger as Morgan swung around,*
> *And sent the grim bushranger blaspheming to the ground.*
>
> *So fell the dread Dan Morgan in Eighteen sixty-five,*
> *In death as much unpitied as hated when alive.*
> *He lived by blood and plunder, an outlaw to the end;*
> *In life he showed no mercy, in death he left no friend.*
> *And all who seek to follow in Morgan's evil track*
> *Should heed the boobook's warning: 'Go back, go back, go back!'*
>
>   Edward Harrington

The police were about to move when the stockman, John Quinlan, stepped from behind a large tree about fifty yards from Morgan. Not renowned for accuracy with his old fowling piece, he nervously took aim. Just as Ewan MacPherson was pointing to a horse and saying, 'That's the one I intend lending you', John Quinlan fired:

Morgan fell, blood gushing from his throat. The bullet had entered behind his shoulder and ploughed upwards tearing through his wind-pipe.

Obviously dying, the bushranger was carried into the woolshed where police and station-hands crowded in to see him. Barely conscious, he refused to answer questions from the police, but called occasionally for water. Just before lapsing into unconsciousness, he rallied sufficiently to ask, 'Why didn't you challenge me, you could have given me a chance.'

To this Ewan MacPherson replied, 'Morgan, you got the same chance you gave your victims.'

About 2 o'clock, Morgan died and a gruesome carnival began. Whatever depths this man's sadism reached during his grisly career, they were now to be surpassed.

The body was propped up on bags and exhibited to the public in a stable beside the Wangaratta gaol. The eyes were opened and one of the two Colt revolvers found on the bushranger was placed in his right hand.

The local photographer, Henry Poil, made the most of the occasion and set up his primitive but elaborate flash gear to take post-card photographs.

Mr Poil's requirements being fully satisfied, Dr Henry of Benalla, using a pocket-knife, cut away the beard tearing skin and flesh from the neck and chin. He declared he would have a tobacco pouch made from the hair. The idea was a popular one and so many locks of hair were souvenired, that the head was nearly bald when the police called a halt and proudly showed the beard around.

Next, the head itself was removed and placed on the chest of the torso. Later, the head was shaved, soaked in brine, then wrapped in hessian and sent to Professor George Halford of Melbourne University for examination.

The Professor later declared that, because the head was poorly preserved, it was too badly decomposed to be of much value to science. Still, a death mask was made for the University's anatomical museum.

As a result of the public outcry against this mutilation, a board of enquiry was set up to look into the affair. Superintendent Cobham was severely reprimanded and reduced in rank.

John Quinlan meanwhile was the hero of the day and he also posed for Mr Poil's camera.

Later, he collected his £1,000 reward for his great luck with the fowling piece, but the money was his only reward. Morgan's last words were to plague his mind for the rest of his days.

When the MacPhersons moved north to Queensland, Quinlan went with them.

Western Queensland was largely settled by pastoralists from Victoria. Ewan Macpherson appears to have bought and sold properties several times before being caught by the lure of Queensland. He sold up everything to stake his fortune in Dagworth, where, after his death, everything was lost in a terrible drought at the turn of the century.

The Macpherson family came to Victoria from Scotland in 1854, taking up land in Northern Victoria and across the Murray in New South Wales.

The family spent a lot of time in Melbourne, especially during the hot summers. Margaret, the youngest, was educated in Melbourne and at least two of the boys went to Scotch College.

By the time Robert Macpherson and his brothers had moved to Queensland, Christina had become a young lady enjoying life in Melbourne with her mother and her sisters, Jean and Margaret.

In 1891, Margaret, the youngest member of the family, married Stewart, later Justice Sir Stewart McArthur of Meningoort, Camperdown. This town is only a short distance from the coastal town of Warrnambool.

It was at the Warrnambool Annual Steeplechase Meeting on 24th April, 1894, that Thomas Bulch's new march *Craigielee* was played for the first time. Less than a year later but many, many miles away to the North, in Winton, Queensland, it would be sung as *Waltzing Matilda* for the Premier of that state.

The Warrnambool Annual Steeplechase Meeting was the premier social event for the Western Districts of Victoria and, as well as being a social must, the meeting provided a great opportunity for family reunions. So, it was natural for Christina to be a guest of her sister,

Margaret and her husband Stewart McArthur at Meningoort, during carnival week.

One reason we may be sure that she was there is that she told many people that the music of *Waltzing Matilda* came from music which she heard played by the band at the Warrnambool Races. She could not be sure of its title, but believed it to be an old Scottish tune or hymn and did not know whether there were any words to it.

The files of *The Warrnambool Standard* confirm in a report on the carnival that the march *Craigielee* was indeed played:

WARRNAMBOOL RACES HELD TUESDAY 24TH AND THURSDAY 26TH APRIL, 1894.
WARRNAMBOOL AMATEUR TURF CLUB 25TH APRIL, 1894.
HIS EXCELLENCY THE GOVERNOR LORD HOPETOUN PRESENT.
MUSIC BY THE TOWN BAND ON TUESDAY, 24th AND THURSDAY 26th APRIL, 1894
March — 'CRAIGIELEE'
Schottische — 'THE ARGYLE'
March — 'JEANNIE GRAY'
Waltz — 'AFTER THE BALL'
Fantasia — OP. 'BOHEMIAN GIRL'
Quadrilles — 'OLD TIMES'
Grand March — 'BRAVE BARNABY'
Serenade — 'TWILIGHT WHISPERINGS'
March — 'THE JACOBITE'

Thomas Bulch's march, *Craigielee*, as published by Lyons' Band Journal, printed in Germany. The march was played for the first time at the Warrnambool Races, April, 1894. It has an introduction of eight bars before the *Waltzing Matilda* theme commences, played by cornets and, from bar 25, by first baritone. Two other melodies follow.

The Annual Steeplechase Meeting, Warrnambool, Victoria, April, 1983.

On 10th October, 1968, Mrs A. J. McIntosh wrote in a letter to the author:

I can confirm that Mrs Stewart McArthur (nee Margaret Macpherson) was my mother and was Christina's sister. I know that Aunt Chris would have been at the Warrnambool Races, maybe in 1894 and many other times, as it was a most natural place for her to be.

The two families (especially the younger members) were close friends, and Meningoort, Camperdown, Victoria, the home of the pioneer Peter McArthur and his large family was a most hospitable and happy home. Margaret married into the family and Chris was a constant visitor and dearly loved.

Warrnambool race week in March was always a gay time and all the families from far and near gathered there, bringing young guests with them and staying in the town.

I know that Christina heard that 'catchy little tune' (as Banjo Paterson later called it) at the Warrnambool Races, played on the lawn by the local band. She did not know the name of it, but she hummed it, and it pleased her and she played it on the piano. She was a most accomplished pianist. Her gift was her very accurate ear for music. To come home and play what she heard was a most natural thing for her to do and in those days, as you would well know, the piano was the centre of life and gaiety.

I can't prove this, as I was only 6 months old in 1894! But I have been brought up with it all my life — Aunt Chris and her clever gift, and her little song which she and Banjo put together and which became so popular all around the woolsheds and riverboats of Queensland and New South Wales.

I heard her play and sing it so often, from my earliest childhood. I can remember Aunt Chris coming to live with us for a while at the turn of the century when she returned from Queensland after Dagworth was lost. From that time onwards she made her home in Melbourne, with a tiny income and modest earnings. She died in 1935 or '36.

As early as the 1914-18 war, her song was well known and must have been published by then, and some of us should have realized that she

'Seemingly endless miles' — **Queensland**

could have been entitled to some of the profits. We must have been very uncommercial!

We were all so familiar with the song and the words put together by these two clever people and Aunt Chris was surprised and happy to hear the general public taking it up.

Finally, I would say there are no 'theories', differing or otherwise in my mind. The tune that Christina heard was adapted to the words created by Banjo and, after much trial and error and great fun, they produced between them 'Waltzing Matilda' — just like any modern team with talent would do today.

I was most interested to see the music, and I return it herewith as I know it must be very valuable.

In December, 1894, Christina's mother died and, soon afterwards, with her father and sister, Jean, she journeyed North to Dagworth.

Arriving by train in Longreach, they travelled on by Cobb and Co. coach. The journey of 110 miles up to Winton on the Western River would have been made quite pleasant by the wonderful condition of the country after a bumper early Wet Season. They would have looked out upon seemingly endless miles of waving green Mitchell grass plains with their wheat-like crop of seed turning gold and bending to the North Wind from the Gulf. Occasionally, the view was broken by coach high flats of peabush, and then out into the open again through a patch of bright yellowbells, stretching away to a flat horizon Eastwards and off to purple hills on the West.

Robert Macpherson met the family in Winton, where they broke their journey before continuing to Dagworth, still a two-day trip away to the North West. During this stopover, Christina met her old friend from schooldays, Sarah Riley.

Sarah was engaged to a handsome young Sydney solicitor whose first book of bush ballads was about to be published, after which he would be known throughout Australia as Banjo Paterson.

Paterson, a Christmas guest of the Rileys, was introduced to Christina and Robert Macpherson. He and Sarah were invited to Dagworth.

33

The Boiling Billy

Visitors to North West Queensland in the Nineties found the area seething with social and political unrest surrounding the Shearers' Strikes of 1891 and 1894. The disturbances associated with these strikes, which the government treated as insurrections, can now be seen as a turning point in Australian history. They would lead to the formation of the Labour Movement and the election of truly representative parliaments.

It has been said that the best national anthems have been written during the white heat of battle, that they emerged from times of national strife or crisis. One can easily think of anthems which fit this description. It is certainly true that anthems cannot be foisted upon a people by decree or by legislation. The true national anthem always has a close association with the social and political evolution of the homeland.

Waltzing Matilda has often been promoted in recent times as a song suitable for national anthem status. These promotions have usually met a wall of opposition which claims that it would be ridiculous for a nation to have as its anthem a frivolous colonial ballad about a sheep-stealing vagrant or tramp — a hobo.

It is equally ridiculous to classify the swagman as a tramp or hobo, for to do so is to express ignorance of the fact that walking and carrying one's swag from job to job was once the norm for bush workers. Ownership of a horse carried considerable status and was often a motive for robbery, sometimes murder.

It will soon become evident to most readers

'The spirit at work underneath the surface.'
Leichardt River

that our song is indeed one of social significance. The reason that this is not often realised by Australians lies in the art of the poet, the balladist, who wrote about current events in such a way that the ballad would live long after those important events were forgotten.

Those important events began at Barcaldine in 1891 when one thousand striking Union shearers went into camp in a scrub near the town and organised themselves in military order and began drilling under the Eureka flag.

There were numerous violent incidents throughout the Central West of Queensland and the authorities, as they did at Eureka in 1854, reacted with considerable force. In the third volume of his *History of Queensland: Its People and Industries*, M. J. Fox writes:

In one of the camps there were 150 rifles in the hands of men who knew how to use them, where determination was expressed that no matter what the outcome might be, free labour from the South must not start work. Police Inspector Ahearn seized powder, ball and shot while it was being transmitted to Clermont by the Labour leaders and obviously the movement meant war. Attempts at incendiarism at Northampton Downs, Maneroo, and elsewhere demonstrated the spirit at work underneath the surface, and attempts at train-wrecking also bore witness to the sinister intentions of rebels, for rebels the law-breakers were. The Government, however, was neither blind nor supine, and although it was not very long before the strike leaders called out 2,000 of the western men, the Defence Force was by that time under arms. A Gatling gun and sixty officers and men, and later fifty members of the Moreton Mounted Infantry were placed under the command of Major Jackson.

Before the shearers realised that facts were against them, there were 1,400 men of the Defence Forces under arms, in addition to hundreds of police, beyond whom there were many special constables, who rendered valuable services. The difficulties of the settlers in the west were largely

'The best national anthems have been written during the white heat of battle.'

Mustering sheep for shearing

increased by the carriers joining the strikers, and there were not less than 120 teams idle at Barcaldine. Lawlessness, however, was not gaining the day, and despite outrages here and there, which were eventually punished, troopers of the Defence Force proved their value, and broke up camps and assemblages of law-breakers.

Men charged with conspiracy and rioting were found guilty and sentenced, the unionist leaders found themselves short of funds, and before long the strike was declared off. After all, the hawks aimed at big quarry, for when the disturbances were well mastered, the plan of campaign was allowed to transpire. It was no less than the seizure of the central district and the establishment there of a Republic. To that end 8,000 workers, with £20,000 as an army chest, had pledged themselves.

Unionists, as well as other historians, took a different view. On 4th April, 1891, *The Worker* (Brisbane) under its headline *The Capitalist Conspiracy* had this to say:

The last fortnight has seen the climax of the capitalistic conspiracy against unionism. With 1,500 or so police and military occupying a few places along the railway lines, the government has felt itself strong enough to invite lawlessness by the wholesale arrest of union officials upon evidently trumped up 'conspiracy' charges. Fortunately, private warning had been given of what might be expected and ample arrangements made for the prevention of all excitement among unionists, for peaceful submission to arrest and for the filling of all offices as officials were arrested. The Barcaldine arrangements in particular were so perfect that half a dozen or half a hundred committees would have been forthcoming in due order had they been required. The preposterous 'conspiracy' charges have thus utterly failed in their purpose and can have no effect but to emphasise the alliance existing between organised Capitalism and the Government.

'The little outback town of Winton gave Australia a national airline and a national song.'

Red kangaroo

In the work *Australia — A Social and Political History*, edited by Professor Gordon Greenwood, R. A. Gollan contributed a chapter entitled *Nationalism, the Labour Movement and the Commonwealth*. He has this to say about the 1891 Strike:

The strike was not an insurrection, even though it appeared so to the employers and large numbers of the public. Many of the shearers were armed, as they always were in the back country, and the large encampments had the appearance of an insurrectionary army. But the significant fact is that there was no bloodshed. There was no insurrection because the shearers were not revolutionaries. They had a profound belief in their rights as trade unionists and there was a widespread socialist ideology, but it was not a revolutionary socialism. The strike was not seen as part of a mass movement directed towards the violent overthrow of the State, but simply as the only available means, under the then conditions, of defending the principle of collective industrial agreements.

Irresponsibles amongst the unionists committed acts of vandalism and provocation, but the responsible leaders appear to have exercised all possible restraint upon their followers. They did not believe in violence, and were also well aware that should it be precipitated by either side, they would be defeated. Nevertheless, as the bitterness of the struggle increased, some revolutionary feeling undoubtedly existed.

Certainly, the shearers flew the defiant, revolutionary Eureka flag and *The Worker*, under William Lane as Editor, printed the rebel-rousing verses of Henry Lawson, including *Freedom on the Wallaby*.

This verse, which subsequently became a song, was read in the Queensland parliament. Henry was branded, with others, as dangerous and subversive. This would have pleased Henry no end, adding another feather to his tattered cap.

Brolgas, or Native Companions

'Just as the fledgling airline was to spread its wings and fly further and further across Australia and then the world, so it was with Matilda.'

However, Henry retreated South to Sydney soon afterwards. Then came the verse debate with Paterson.

It is therefore very likely that Paterson was shown *Freedom on the Wallaby* and told of its official reception in Brisbane. As mentioned earlier, it can be seen that Lawson may have had a finger in the Matilda pie:

> *She's going to light another fire*
> *And boil another billy.*

Indeed, another fire was lit with a riot by shearers at Oondooroo Station, near Winton, on 3rd July, 1894. The billy came to the boil the following night when the nearby Ayrshire Downs woolshed was burned down. Again the West was in turmoil over the principle of *Freedom of Contract*, under which the pastoralists could employ non-Union labour as well as affording them considerable latitude in setting conditions. Once again, violence became commonplace and a brief summary from official records shows the following incidents:

8th and 9th July	— serious intimidation at Milo, Adavale.
14th July	— robbery of a hawker's stores.
16th and 17th July	— inflammatory leaflets circulated, Barcaldine district.
20th July	— at Coombemartin during signing of the roll, a unionist, Prior, shot another unionist named Ashford.
25th July	— Redcliffe woolshed and 84 bales of wool destroyed.
25th July	— violence at Hughenden.
26th July	— violence at Adavale.
27th July	— intimidation at Hughenden.
30th July	— a free labourer assaulted.
2nd August	— Cambridge Downs woolshed burned.

Dingoes

5th August	— intimidation at Alice Downs.
8th August	— Murweh woolshed destroyed.
13th August	— Eroungella woolshed destroyed, and a constable in charge left bound to a tree by the marauders.
10th and 13th August	— cases of intimidation were reported.
16th August	— grass burned on Malvern Hills Station.
23rd August	— Cassilis woolshed destroyed.
27th August	— Manuka woolshed destroyed.
2nd September	— Dagworth woolshed was surrounded by an armed band of about sixteen, shots exchanged and the shed burned.

Brolgas on a lignum waterhole

Was *Waltzing Matilda* with its swagman and his billy on the boil Paterson's symbolic answer to Lawson's *Freedom on the Wallaby*?

This is a question to keep in mind as we look at the history of the weeks immediately preceding the birth of the song. If the answer is yes, then it explains why the poet himself had so little to say concerning the circumstances which surrounded the origins of the song. Knowing his feelings for the bush worker, his political inclinations and his acknowledged reticence, while realising that he was a respected Sydney solicitor moving in the best circles, we can be certain that Paterson would not want the notoriety which Lawson earned with *Freedom on the Wallaby*.

Was the swagman's billy just a billy? Was the jumbuck just one of many thousands of sheep? What of the squatter and policemen? Why such overwhelming force to arrest one man? Is *Waltzing Matilda* just a frivolous ballad or is it an allegory? Is the song symbolic of great social conflict which we have chosen to forget but which the ghost of a swagman calls us to remember?

Emu

FREEDOM ON THE WALLABY

Australia's a big country
   An' freedom's humping bluey.
An freedom's on the wallaby,
   Oh don't you hear her coo-ee?
She's just begun to boomerang,
   She'll knock the tyrants silly,
She's goin' to light another fire
   And boil another billy.

Our fathers toiled for bitter bread,
   While loafers thrived beside 'em,
But food to eat and clothes to wear,
   Their native land denied 'em.
An' so they left their native land
   In spite of their devotion,
An' so they came, or if they stole,
   Were sent across the ocean.

Then Freedom couldn't stand the glare
   Of royalty's regalia,
She left the loafers where they were
   An' came out to Australia.
But now across the mighty main
   The chains have come ter bind her,
She little thought to see again
   The wrongs she left behind her.

Our parents toiled to make a home,
   Hard grubbin' 'twas an' clearin',
They wasn't crowded much with lords
   When they was pioneerin';
But now that we have made the land
   A garden full of promise,
Old Greed must crook 'is dirty hand
   And come ter take it from us.

So we must fly the rebel flag
   As others did before us,
And we must sing the rebel song
   And join in rebel chorus,
We'll make the tyrants feel the sting
   O' those that they would throttle;
They needn't say the fault is ours,
   If blood shall stain the wattle.

Henry Lawson
1891

'Freedom's on the wallaby —
don't you hear her coo-ee?'

Grey doe kangaroo and joey

FROM THE SOUTH TO THE NORTH

There are anxious watching faces
   'mongst the workers of the South.
There's a hope in many bosoms,
   there's a prayer in many a mouth.
We are waiting for the issues as the
   moments bring them forth.
As we send a hearty greeting to our
   brothers in the North.

From the dirty, smokey city; from the
   workshop and the mine,
We stretch the hand of friendship
   'cross the distant border line,
For we feel the Cause is mighty and
   the truth can never fail.
If we're true to one another Truth
   and Justice must prevail.

So we watch the battle keenly,
   Counting out the leaden hours,
For we know the stake at issue and
   their victory is ours.
In the name of Holy Freedom, in the
   name of Truth and Right,
We applaud their noble efforts and
   we'll help them in the fight.

For the sake of wife and mother, for
   the children yet unborn,
Close the ranks a little longer, leave
   the tyrants' sheep unshorn.
If the time arrives for action we can
   also go and dare,
And we have a little money and a
   man or two to spare.
So I send a friendly greeting o'er the
   border line to you,
Tell the North to stand together, for
   the South is staunch and true.

Edwin J. Brady

The Jumbuck

"Righto, men," called Neil Highland, as he swung into his saddle, "it's time to move. The clouds are rolling up and we want our work done tonight before any rain falls."

"Yes," Moody agreed, "we've waited a long time for this and I reckon those clouds are a good omen. It will be a dark night, so let's go and light it up for those squatter Macpherson bastards and their scabs and blacklegs."

"Got your matches ready, Frenchy?" Bill Gumley asked over his shoulder, as he tightened the girth on his bay gelding.

"You look to your work, Gumley, and I'll look to mine." Frenchy Hoffmeister snarled back with a wave of the letter which he had received on yesterday's mail coach. "Just make sure that you shoot straight all you chaps and give me plenty of covering fire. I don't want to be a sitting duck when I set that shed alight."

"We'll give it to 'em, won't we mates?" cried Chris Connolly. There came a general call of enthusiastic agreement, as Connolly doused the campfire.

"I still reckon," muttered Lewis Murray, "we should wait until tomorrow night, like we were told in the letter."

"Just pick up your rifle, Murray, and get on that bag o' bones that passes for a horse. He might just make it to the Dagworth shed. It's all of sixteen miles, so let's get cracking."

Now, Ted Dempsey gave voice to his doubts: "Don't forget mates that there's a thousand pounds reward on all our heads once this shed goes up. What if it does rain? They'll be able to track us to Kingdom Come."

"All the more reason to move quickly now," offered Jack Crimmins, who was supported by a gruff "yes" from his mate, Jim Spellacy.

There was no more dissension. In any case, Highland, Moody and Goode had already ridden off and were now rounding the end of the waterhole below their camp on the Fourmile.

These unionists had been gathering here,

'Down came a jumbuck...'

arriving in groups of two and three, since the arrival of the mail coach at Kynuna on Friday. Word had come that Macpherson had mustered sheep ready to commence shearing on Monday with non-union, 'scab' labour. They had been ordered to attack the Dagworth shed on Sunday night. The threat of rain had forced this decision to move tonight.

Now, sixteen men were riding East into the gathering dark along the channels of the Diamantina River, determined that there would be no shearing at Dagworth on Monday.

At the shed were Bob Macpherson and twenty men, including his brothers, Jack and Gideon, overseer, Henry Dyer, shed overseer, Weldon Tomlin, and a police constable, Michael Daly.

Shearing should have begun at Dagworth on 15th August, but no men turned up to sign the '94 Agreement, the subject of the present strike. Bob Macpherson had called for help from the police in guarding the shed against attacks such as had occurred elsewhere. For five weeks now, a constable had been stationed there.

With sheep mustered and a team of 'free labourers' recruited to begin shearing on Monday, the station men were prepared for an attack. Six sheds had already been destroyed in the district, the last at Manuka only four days earlier.

Tonight, Saturday, 1st September, all was quiet, as the Macphersons and their men doused their camp lights and retired to stretchers in several iron huts near the shed. No sign of union activity had been reported anywhere in the district. Two policemen stationed in Kynuna were keeping a close watch on movements in the large union camp in that town. So, the Dagworth people felt reasonably secure and were confident that shearing would at last get under way. A threat of rain presented the only doubt and 140 weaner lambs had been penned in the woolshed for shelter should rain fall during the night.

On watch at midnight were Weldon Tomlin and Constable Daly. The station dogs began to bark and both watchmen checked their perimiters and conferred. Neither had seen or heard anything above the rustle of a light northerly breeze through coolibah leaves and the drone of a million crickets which drifted with the breeze through the dark, cloudy night.

The approaching union shearers, now on foot, also heard the dogs. Half an hour earlier, they had left their horses when two scouts returned to

Coolibahs at sunset

Merino sheep, Cranbourne, Yelarbon.

'Sixteen men riding into the gathering dark along the channels of the Diamantina . . .'

report that it appeared only two men were on watch at the shed.

"Those bloody dogs can hear or smell us on the wind," Highland spoke softly to Moody. "Pass the word back to follow us up this gully until we reach the high ground on the downs side of the shed. Goode, you tell Frenchy to sneak down along the river to the shed. He must be at the shed as soon as we open fire in about half an hour. They'll be confused for a while and that's when he must get into the shed."

Soon, Goode returned to report that Frenchy had moved off towards the shed muttering something unintelligible.

"Well, that's how he got the job." Highland said. "He's a bit mad, but he'll do as he's told."

Soon, the raiders were in a good position on the side of a broken gully to the South of the woolshed. This location commanded a good view, although it was very dark and the shed could only dimly be discerned against the coolibahs on the river.

They waited, watching, to give Frenchy plenty of time to reach his position. It was half an hour past midnight when Highland spoke, "All right now, men, when I fire, you all fire one shot in your own time. Spellacy and Crimmins — you put a few shots through their huts to let them know we mean business."

All at once, the calm of the night was shattered by the report of a shot from Highland's rifle and the ragged volley which followed. As each man fired, he again took cover behind the high bank of the gully. Their position was ideal.

Some answering shots came now from the direction of the huts and one of the unionists yelled, "Put up your arms you bastards or die!"

More shots replied from near the huts and from a point between them and the shed. "Come on, boys," cried Highland, "give it to the bastards. We have waited long enough for this and now we'll have it."

"Rally up, boys, and let them have it," called another.

"Put your arms up you bastards or die!"

"You'll die or we'll die!"

The defenders replied with another volley of bullets aimed at flashes from the rifles of the unionists. Bullets thudded into the creek bank or whined overhead far across the downs country into the night.

Now there came a flash of light from the shed itself. Frenchy had lit his match and very soon the kerosene blazed up.

"Keep firing, men. Don't let the bastards near that fire. We'll soon be able to see anyone who moves. Keep them pinned down."

Constable Daly, armed with a carbine and fifty-nine rounds was standing between the shed and the nearest hut when the first shots blasted through the night. One shot hit the hut and Daly dropped to the ground as several more hissed close by him.

Daly fired two shots before running to the shelter of a large heap of earth nearer the shed. He could near Tomlin returning the fire of the attacking party which he estimated to be forty to fifty yards distant. Firing several more rounds, he then made a dash for the hut occupied by the Macpherson brothers and Henry Dyer.

"How many of them are there?" asked Bob, as Daly rushed into the hut.

"At least a dozen of them, probably more."

"Take Mr Dyer with you. Gideon, where is that bloody revolver? We can't strike a light. I'll join you as soon as we find it. Make for the shed if you can."

Daly and Dyer made a dash for the mound of earth where they were joined by Tomlin. They fired seven or eight shots each before there was a flash of light and then a flare from the shed.

Bob Macpherson dropped beside the other defenders. "They've lit the shed, the mongrels. Aim around the fire while I try to make it to the side of the shed. The lambs! We've got to get the lambs out. That fire is taking hold quickly."

Bob made a dash for the shed, but a hail of bullets from the raiders on the creek bank made him drop for cover. As more bullets thudded into the earth around him and into the wall of the shed, he was forced to retreat for cover to where the others were returning fire from the protection of the mound of earth. The shed now well ablaze, flames were racing across the greasy floor and leaping up the walls and uprights into the roof structure. It was already too late to save the lambs and some bales of wool stored in the shed.

As the rain of bullets continued, there was nothing the defenders could do apart from returning the fire of the raiders. Whoever had set the shed alight was well clear by now.

"Keep firing!" yelled Constable Daly. "Forget about the shed. We mustn't let them make a charge for the huts."

45

'. . . determined there would be no shearing at Dagworth on Monday.'

"Yes, there's no saying they won't burn them too," said Bob. "Watch the hut where the woman and children are. It's too late to save the shed and the lambs. You're right, Daly, we must keep them pinned down in that gully."

As Bob finished speaking, the roof of the woolshed fell in with an eruption of flame sending a huge fireball roaring into the night sky, lighting up all the huts and sheepyards, as well as the coolibahs along the river. Some of the raiders who had evidently crept much closer than the defenders realised could be seen running for the shelter of the gully.

When the roof settled, there was silence. The raiders had gone. Their work was done.

Soon, it began to rain, first as a drizzle and then steadily enough to extinguish the fire, but, by this time, only a small corner of the woolshed remained.

All that Bob Macpherson could do now was instruct one of his men to run the horses in at first light, so that a search could be made for the attacking party and a message sent to the telegraph station at Ayrshire for relay to the police in Winton and the Colonial Secretary in Brisbane.

Soon news of the fire at Dagworth would be blazing through the Southern press. Every incident in this uprising of the swagmen shearers in North West Queensland made news across the continent at a time when the states were striving to minimise their differences in the interests of the movement for Federation.

Nobody was then to know that this was to be the last serious incident of the 1894 Shearers' Strike. State and local authorities would react strongly and quickly to this latest outrage — the burning of not just a woolshed and bales of wool, but the incineration of more than a hundred young jumbucks at Dagworth.

Running the horses at dawn...

'...so that a search could be made for the attacking party.'

The Swagman and Policemen

Dawn on Sunday brought fine weather. At first light Bob Macpherson and Constable Daly attempted to track the raiders without success, for the rain had been sufficient to obliterate all tracks. However, they were at least able to ascertain that the unionists had travelled upstream towards Kynuna, because they had left several gates open.

Returning to the scene of last night's rifle battle, Macpherson and Daly gathered a number of cartridges, full and empty, from the bed of the gully and from there to within ten yards of the shed. These were mainly Winchester, some Martini Henry and some revolver cartridges.

Bullets were also recovered from several of the huts. (See appendices A and B)

News of the attack having reached Winton, a party of police was already preparing to ride to Dagworth, while details were being transmitted to authorities in the South. However, as it would be some time before the Winton police party reached Dagworth, Macpherson with Daly and others, rode the twenty miles to the town of Kynuna to enlist the aid of Senior Constable Austin Cafferty and the other policeman stationed there. Here some interesting news awaited them.

There was little movement until midday at the

'A number of strange horses . . .
seen westwards towards the ranges.'

Dagworth Hills

Main channel, Diamantina River

temporary union camp by the waterhole four miles from Kynuna. Only eight of the party which attacked the woolshed were still in camp.

These eight gathered for a midday meal of corned mutton and damper, after which it was planned that they too would break camp and go their separate ways. Yarning quietly, most expressed confidence that they could not be connected with events at Dagworth, because the rain had so thoroughly covered their tracks. If questioned, they need only stick fast to their story that nobody had left the camp during the night.

Only Frenchy Hoffmeister showed any signs of real concern. With a thousand pounds reward on his head after setting fire to the woolshed, it would be strange for any man not to show the strain and Frenchy was known to be a bit barmy at the best of times. Now, overnight, as he well knew, he had become the most wanted man in the country. Perhaps the burning of so many helpless lambs in their pens also weighed heavily on his mind today.

After dinner, Frenchy began to behave in a very distressed manner, striding up and down through the camp for some time. Eventually, he returned to the fire where the others sat talking.

There Hoffmeister took from his pocket a letter which he dropped into the fire. He stood watching until it was completely burned and then said, "That done, I'm satisfied." Then he strode away from the group once more, moving off down towards the waterhole.

Soon afterwards, those remaining at the campfire were startled by the report of a gunshot from the direction in which Frenchy had walked.

Highland called to ask what Frenchy was shooting at and, there being no reply, went to see for himself. He found Frenchy lying on the ground with blood running from his mouth. He was dead. His rifle lay beside him and there was a revolver near his hand.

Highland called to the others and, after they had all recovered from the initial shock of finding

Coolibah billabong, Diamantina River

their comrade dead, there was a discussion about the immediate implications of this sudden tragedy. Should they report the death, or should they all decamp at once?

The bonds of mateship prevailed and it was eventually decided that Neil Highland should ride over to Kynuna Station and report Hoffmeister's death to the manager, Mr McCowan.

Arriving at Kynuna soon after McCowan reported the apparent suicide to Senior Constable Cafferty, the Dagworth party were given the news. The two policemen from Kynuna now joined Constable Daly and squatter, Bob Macpherson, in riding to the Fourmile where Hoffmeister had suicided.

So, we find three policemen riding together in a land where, to this day, there has seldom been more than one.

Arriving at the union camp, the three policemen and squatter Macpherson inspected Frenchy's body near the waterhole. Daly noted that the rifle had recently been fired and that Frenchy's cartridges were the same as some of the empty shells recovered early that morning near the Dagworth woolshed.

All seven unionists were now arrested and escorted to Kynuna where they would be detained pending an inquest to be held on Wednesday before the Police Magistrate, Ernest Eglinton.

Much of the evidence given at the inquest was conflicting, especially that given by the unionists concerning Hoffmeister's movements and his associations with others in the group. Lies were told about ownership of the revolver which was found with Frenchy's body and it was stated that this was the only rifle seen in the camp.

Initially the police suspected that Hoffmeister had been wounded at the Dagworth affray, but Doctor Wellford's statement ruled this out. He stated that the fatal bullet had entered through the roof of Hoffmeister's mouth and that his teeth would have been shattered if another person had fired the shot.

(See appendices C and D)

'It seems he had a particular incident in mind.'

The Squatter

The Southern press carried detailed accounts of events at Dagworth. Communications were slow by today's standards and a report despatched from Winton on 13th September, appeared in the Brisbane *Courier* on the 20th:

'The enquiry into the death of Hoffmeister at a union camp at Kynuna resulted in a verdict of suicide. Found with him were a rifle and sixty-eight cartridges and a revolver and twenty empty cartridge shells. He committed suicide at a camp which had been formed four miles this side of Kynuna, some distance from the main camp, and about fourteen miles from the Dagworth shed. They gave as their reason for forming a camp there that the grass was better, but I am informed that there is good grass around the township. The significant part of the business is that there is a track from this camp to the woolshed, which forms something like one side of a triangle, and does not, therefore, go near the head station.'

Another report states that all the men found with Hoffmeister had served prison sentences.

On 1st December, a man named Tierney was brought before the bench in Winton charged in connection with the Dagworth outrage. He was discharged when police offered no evidence, Macpherson and Tomlin being unable to recognize his voice.

On 5th November (Guy Fawkes Day) an Inspector Cooper searched Kynuna for arms and ammunition. He seized two breech loading guns, three Winchester rifles, one revolver, 2495 Winchester cartridges, thirty-three pounds of powder, and a large quantity of shot and detonators. A strong recommendation was made for the establishment of a police station at Kynuna.

The fact that there had not been even one policeman stationed in the Kynuna district on a permanent basis prior to these events highlights Paterson's extraordinary use of three policemen with the squatter to arrest one terrified swagman. It seems that he had a particular incident in mind.

In subsequent confidential reports, the names of several men suspected of having been involved in the Dagworth fire are given. No convictions are recorded.

Shearing began at Dagworth in November and continued well into December. Police were still stationed at the shed, as can be seen in a photograph taken at the time. The building in the photograph appears to be one of the huts adapted to serve as an emergency woolshed.

There was still need for caution as can be seen in a telegram from Winton on 10th December. This reads in part:

'Have information tonight from Dagworth large tract country on fire westward towards ranges. Also number strange horses were seen in same direction two days before Dagworth shed burnt. I am carefully watching that party's portion of district and have great hopes. Please do not mention this'.

This caution was well warranted, as were the fortifications made at Dagworth woolshed. Soon after the foregoing telegram was sent, there came another attack. This time there were only three men, perhaps an advance party, and after a brief engagement these were driven off. Shearing was then completed without further harassment.

So, we come to the end of 1894, a year which stands out as the most exciting in the history of the Winton district. The unionists lost the battle, but the cost to the squatters, despite strong police reinforcements, the swearing in of eighty special constables and a reward of one thousand pounds, was considerable. The loss, in sheds alone, was £15,000. This was a very large sum of money in those times.

It was a wild year, but one cannot help wondering whether, despite all the bitterness, bushmen would not kill bushmen.

Ewan Macpherson, having just lost his wife, would have been a very relieved man when he arrived at Dagworth with Christina and Jean to find the troubles over and his sons, Bob, Jack and

Three policemen with squatter, Bob Macpherson, his brothers and other men at a defensive stockade, Dagworth Station, 1894. A band of swagmen-shearers burned the woolshed and 140 sheep here on 1st September in that year. 'Banjo' Paterson wrote 'Waltzing Matilda' at Dagworth a few months later.

Gideon, all hale and hearty.

Soon after this reunion of the Macpherson family, the engaged couple, Sarah Riley and Barty Paterson arrived. In those days, the buggy ride from Winton to Dagworth took two days and it is on record that the couple spent the night with the Morrisons at Ayrshire Downs, a property which gave its name to the spectacular limestone hills through which the road still passes.

The Morrisons and Macphersons were great friends and Sarah Riley had been governess to the Morrison children. So, it was quite natural for Mrs Morrison to accompany the young couple to Dagworth as chaperon.

Paterson spent about three weeks at Dagworth and, going by reports from those who remembered, enjoyed his stay immensely. While the attraction for him at Winton was certainly Sarah Riley, we may be quite sure that his interest in visiting Dagworth centred on the recent stormy events associated with the Shearers' Strike. This is borne out by the fact that he wrote about the burning of the Dagworth woolshed on his return to Sydney and he records the incident in his book, *Three Elephant Power*. (See appendix I)

Paterson's love for the bush, for horses and riding, was shared by his host, Bob Macpherson, who ran a fine string of horses. One of their first rides would have been to the scene of the attack by the rebel shearers, where the poet would have been given a graphic account of the affray.

Another point of interest was the nearby Scour Hole, where the wool was washed. Close to the Scour Hole, Paterson was shown a lonely grave marked by a solitary gidgea post. Some years ago, this post was still there and it marks the resting place of George Hamlyn Pope, woolscourer. Pope drowned in the Scour Hole on the night of 17th September, 1891. Workmates last saw him late that night, drunk, in his tent. These men, Thomas Richardson, scour hand, and Benjamin Brett, wool roller, with scour overseer, Jacob Woods, gave evidence at an inquest conducted by Robert Macpherson, J.P., on 29th September, 1891. (See appendix E)

Pope's death is the only drowning recorded in the district between the first settlement and Paterson's visit. The only recorded suicide is that of Samuel Hoffmeister.

The Dagworth country was in fine condition, so

that visitors in January, 1895, looked out across miles of undulating downs covered with lush green Mitchell and Flinders grasses. Four and a half inches of rain had fallen in November and December, making a total of thirty inches, where the annual average is only sixteen. January and February bringing a further thirteen inches, the Macphersons and their visitors would have spent some days confined to the homestead.

Dagworth at this time covered a quarter of a million acres and, as the men spent the long summer days mustering and inspecting the wide plains, Barty Paterson plied Bob Macpherson with many questions.

'How many sheep are you running here now, Bob?'

'Well, there have been a few comings and goings lately. We've just bought 15,000 young wethers for 2/6 from Oondooroo and 11,500 breeding ewes from Lorne at 2/-. When these are delivered and we've sent off 20,000 wethers and 11,000 cull ewes which are sold, there will be about 120,000 head. All in all, with the lambing coming up from 57,000 breeders we hope to have over 150,000 by shearing time in September.'

'That's a lot of stock Bob; you've got a lot of feed but what's the water situation later in the year?'

'Well, Barty, normally we've been running a lot less. For the last two years we've had Penola leased on the other side of Kynuna and a lot of the stock have been over there. Now, with so much feed here, we've brought nearly all the Penola sheep home to save costs. That's why Jack Carter's here. He's really overseer at Penola and my brother Jack is Dagworth overseer.

'As for water, we've dammed the river up on the Kynuna boundary with stone overshots — a big job, Mick Fahey did it for us — wonderful permanent billabongs up there now. One day we'll show it to you as it's really something to see. Also last year we sank a flowing bore out on the Wombat block and this will be a valuable asset later in the year.'

'What about cattle and horses?'

'Yes, there's just over 300 head of cattle and

'Mustering the wide plains.'

Carisbrook Hills, Winton.

plenty of horses. We'll see you don't run short of fresh mounts — there's about 450 of them and, though I say so myself, they're a fine lot too'.

'And where do you get your rams? This must be a problem when you're so far from the studs?'

'Yes, it has always been a problem up here but I think we're over it now. We've just bought 200 three guinea stud ewes, twenty-seven rams at twenty-five guineas and one for 200 guineas from F. S. Faulkner, Moonbria. These are splendid sheep and should prove a good investment. Added to the station studs, we can breed our own rams in future.'

'And I suppose with the increase in numbers you've had to increase your work force. Is the whole property run from the homestead or are there outstations?'

'Well, until now it's all been handled from the homestead with temporary camps outside at times. This year we'll be putting up two huts out on the run, one with a set of drafting yards and a paddock for the studs. There'll be another men's hut going up at the station too. Since we've employed the two married couples, accommodation is pretty heavily taxed. Apart from Jack, Gideon, Carter and the book-keeper inside, there are ten men plus the cook and the gardener.'

'I suppose, the season being so good, the woolclip will be a good one.'

'Yes. Of course, if we don't have any more shearing trouble and we shear on time in September, there will be only ten or eleven months' growth. Still, the grown sheep should cut two and a half pounds dry scoured wool.'

'And Bob, how much would it cost to run Dagworth for a year if that's not being too inquisitive?'

'Well now, the droving will push things up a bit this year. The ewes cost about sixpence a head to deliver and the wethers a penny. Still, apart from improvements the total cost should be just under £9000. Against this, with the wool bringing a shilling a pound, we should have a wool cheque of £14,000 and there could be £6000 from sheep sales, making £20,000 all told. That sounds quite a lot; it's a big increase on previous years,

Aboriginal stockmen

but of course, we have a big debt to pay off on the new bore and the Combo overshots. Hold on there — over this way — a dead sheep I think.'

There is a strange sixth sense which allows a bushman to tell from a considerable distance whether a sheep is dead, sick, or merely sleeping. At this time, with conditions being so good, dead sheep were few and far between. So it was easy for Bob to see signs of an unnatural death.

He called to the blackboy riding with them, 'Here Jimmy, hop off and turn that weaner over.'

Sure enough, when the boy did as he was told, a shoulder and a leg were found to be missing. The sheep had been killed and part of the carcase taken. The skin and the lower legs had been replaced with the untouched side left uppermost.

Paterson asked. 'Who would have done that. Bob? Does it happen often?'

'Oh yes, it is going on all the time — Jimmy put the billy on, we'll have dinner here — yes Barty — bloody bagmen; they're too damned tired to come up to the station and ask for meat so they help themselves. Of course, since the strike, a lot of them won't go near a homestead. The chaps with the dogs are the worst at it and it's not just the sheep they kill, that's the trouble — at lambing time they must mis-mother a hell of a lot of lambs. Of course it's such a waste too as they can't carry the whole carcase. They just take enough for a good feed on the spot and what they can salt and carry in the tuckerbag, or tuckerchute, whichever you like to call it.'

'Well,' said Banjo, 'tuckerbag will do for me. There's no doubt about us Australians, we never seem to be satisfied with one name for anything.'

Certainly, for the size of our population, we have made a remarkable contribution of slang and nick-names to the English language.

Just as pioneering landholders were called squatters and unemployed or itinerant bush workers were swagmen or bagmen, so sheep were called jumbucks.

There are two plausible explanations for the derivation of this term. It appears that, in various

*'Jimmy, put the billy on —
we'll have dinner here.'*

dialects, the aborigine's name for a white mist preceding a shower was *jimba, jombok, dumbock* and *dumbog*. Seemingly, on first seeing a flock of sheep, they could only liken them to such a mist.

One anthropologist who compiled a vocabulary of native languages listed the word *jumbuck* as a verb meaning to communicate, ask or speak. This being so, then because sheep in a mob are continuously bleating and since most Australian animals are mute, it was quite feasible for them to call these talkative animals jumbucks.

Today, this nick-name has been replaced by *monkey* of which the derivation is fairly obvious, but certainly, back in the Nineties *jumbuck* was used occasionally.

Not all of Paterson's rides on Dagworth took him along the shady river. There were many long rides out across the rolling downs, for some parts of the run were twenty-five miles from the homestead. At the end of a long day in the saddle, having let the tired horses go, the men would stroll down for a bogey in one of the many waterholes before dressing for dinner.

After the meal they usually all lingered, talking around the table. In those days, and it's still much the same, conversation was the main form of entertainment. This was before the era of the gramophone and Dagworth boasted no piano. Sometimes, the evening hours would be spent in reading books or newspapers, notably the Bushman's Bible that was *The Sydney Bulletin* as well as the weekly *Queenslander*.

Now there were visitors at Dagworth and the party was a large one, so the books and papers were not needed.

With the western districts still simmering down from the turmoil of recent months and the rifle battle not long past, events of the strike were naturally foremost in conversation. Visitors would insist on a detailed account of the happenings.

Paterson for one was most interested.

On the still summer nights when it was too hot to go to bed early, chairs were taken outside to what today would be the front lawn. In those days, when water had to be carted from the river by dray, there was no such thing as a lawn.

Banjo would be called upon to recite, for this was also one of the popular pastimes.

Although there was no piano, there was an autoharp at Dagworth, a zither-type instrument left there by J. T. Wilson, the book-keeper, who was away on holidays. It didn't take Christina long to master this instrument and she was soon able to play well-known tunes while the others gathered around and sang.

One tune, which Christina was continually playing and humming, enthralled *The Banjo*.

Wildflowers and rolling downs, Winton district

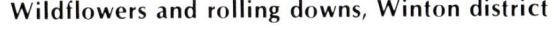

The Billabong

In 1895, the vast holding that was Dagworth was bounded on its Western side by another huge property, Kynuna Station, which gave its name to the settlement on the Northern side of the Diamantina River which grew from a teamsters' camp.

Kynuna Station, owned by Edmund Jowett, was managed by Samuel McColl McCowan, a former partner of Macpherson and Company at Dagworth. Sam had been managing Kynuna for nine years by this time and had become very friendly with Jean Macpherson. These two married later, on 16th April, 1896.

Dagworth and Kynuna Stations were twenty miles apart — quite a handicap to a courtship in the horse and buggy days. So it was that parties from the two stations often met for picnics at a waterhole on their boundary across the Diamantina. At least one such picnic was held during Paterson's stay.

This waterhole, or billabong, remains a pleasant picnic and camping spot today, an oasis of shady coolibah trees where travellers can rest from the long stage across seemingly endless miles of open downs country. Here they may boil the billy while listening to the calls of hundreds of bush birds which make the *Combo* their home.

The *Combo* is really a series of billabongs enlarged from their natural form by a magnificent system of man-made stone overshots, or

'Combo Billabong's shady coolibahs —
an oasis for hundreds of bush birds.'

Corellas

weirs. The contractor employed by Macphersons for this masterpiece of bush engineering was Mickey Fahey. Many Chinese coolies were employed on this work. Mickey Fahey could neither read nor write, yet became known as the *King of Kynuna*, owning much of the town, including an hotel. Mickey did his book-keeping with a set of stones.

So, in 1895, there was an ideal meeting place on the boundary between the two properties. Although there are several waterholes here, one in particular is still referred to as *The Combo Hole*. It is located on the Southern side of the main channel and is indeed the perfect example of a billabong, this being another aboriginal name for dead or still water. This referred to water trapped in outer channels (anabranches) when floodwaters had receded, while the river itself might still be running.

Paterson would certainly have known this term but, on seeing such an array of artifical billabongs, he must certainly have been impressed, just as visitors are today. Here, coolibahs may be seen at their best, providing many shady picnic spots and campsites for fishermen who come to bob their corks for Yellowbelly.

Folklore of the Kynuna-Winton district insists that it was at The Combo that Bob Macpherson related details of a local incident which became the story of *Waltzing Matilda*.

This folklore concerning origins of the song in the district became the foundation on which the author based his five years of research into the history of *Waltzing Matilda* from 1966 to 1971. Because this folklore, supported by years of painstaking research, is pertinent to what is to follow in the next chapter, it is important for the reader to know that the author's grandfather was a friend of Bob Macpherson. He had settled on Rosevale Station, thirty miles to the North of Kynuna and shared Bob Macpherson's interest in horses, especially fast ones. They were both members of the Kynuna Race Club Committee. It was after one of their meetings, while they were enjoying a *Shilling In Shout* that Bob Macpherson dropped dead in the Kynuna Hotel. Bob is buried beside his brother, Jack, near the present Dagworth homestead.

At the beginning of this century, a severe drought devastated the North West plains and Macphersons lost Dagworth to their mortgagees, The Australian Estates Company. Bob, the pioneer squatter, left with only his buckboard and his swag. He was to manage Coolulah and other stations to the North, before returning in his old age to be supervisor of the rabbit netting fence in the Kynuna area. His brother Gideon, who went completely blind, was allowed a grace and favour home at Dagworth for many years. He was buried as a pauper in Toowong Cemetery, Brisbane, in 1930.

Another link of the *Waltzing Matilda* legend came to the author through his family from Jack Carter, who was overseer at Dagworth for Macphersons when the song was written. Jack's nephews, Bruce and Bill, both married members of the Magoffin family. The Carter story, while adding detail, confirms that told by Bob Macpherson to the author's grandfather.

The fact that Bob Macpherson told the story at Combo to Paterson was confirmed by another pioneer, Mrs Jane Black. She recorded a visit to Dagworth in 1897. Calling there with her husband on their way to take over management of Kynuna Station in 1897, Bob Macpherson told them the circumstances surrounding the writing of the song two years earlier. On the strength of his story, they detoured to see Combo on their way to Kynuna. (See appendix F)

Combo is certainly associated with our song, yet there is no record of any drowning there, suicidal or otherwise, and this billabong is neither very deep nor wide.

Perhaps then, the story related by Macpherson at that picnic concerned the recent suicide of Samuel Hoffmeister, swagman-shearer, just eight miles upstream?

What seems most pertinent is that Hoffmeister's death was first reported to Sam McCowan at Kynuna Station and McCowan was certainly present at the picnic. He would have elaborated on any account of the suicide by Bob Macpherson.

What was the story which the great bush balladist heard that day under the shade of a coolibah tree by the placid Combo waters on the Diamantina? Today, as we pass by that billabong, the ghost of a long forgotten bushman calls us to think upon it, but only the ghosts of the men who lived through those far from placid days can know.

'Once...under the shade of a coolibah tree.'

Combo Billabong, Diamantina River, April, 1983. Overshot dams built by Chinese labour nearly a century ago are in danger of being lost unless they are repaired as part of our national heritage.

The Song

The night on which *Waltzing Matilda* was written was little different from any other at Dagworth homestead, this isolated settlement in the frontier country of Western Queensland.

The party seated around the dinner table was a large one. Present that night were Ewan Macpherson and his three sons, Bob, Jack and Gideon, and his daughters, Chris and Jean, with Sarah Riley and Barty Paterson, Kenneth Morrison, Edward Blurton, and the relieving book-keeper, Drysdale.

If there were others, there is no record of their presence. Of course, should we believe every statement made regarding who was present when the song was written, then Dagworth homestead must have resembled the Sydney Opera House. The dimensions of the homestead, which may still be seen from the few weatherworn stumps remaining today, indicate that the dining room would have been quite crowded with the foregoing company.

One more was to join the group when they had finished dinner. They were sitting, talking, when the overseer, Jack Carter arrived, having ridden in late from his day out on the run.

As the overseer sat down, Bob Macpherson asked him, "Well, Mr Carter, what did you see today?"

"Nothing much," said Carter, "only a bagman waltzing Matilda down along the river."

Bob Macpherson had asked an ordinary question and received an ordinary answer, yet it was to have world wide effects far into the future.

"Mr Carter, you said you saw a bagman waltzing Matilda. What does *waltzing Matilda* mean?" asked Barty Paterson.

"Well, you see, Mr Paterson, a bagman or swagman never carries more than he has to, especially out here where distances between settlements are so great. It's a warm climate too, so he doesn't need much nap or clothes. He takes just the minimum — a sugar bag for his tucker, a billy can, and usually he leads a waterbag by a stick poked through a couple of lugs. His swag being fairly thin and light, he carries it over one shoulder by a couple of straps around the middle so that each end hangs loose. Nearly everywhere this is called *humping bluey*, most bush blankets being blue, or *humping the drum*, but in these parts they call it *waltzing Matilda.*"

"Perhaps one swagman seeing another pick up his swag likened it to a man taking a dancing partner," suggested Jack Carter.

"The expression is used still in Victoria too," said Ewan Macpherson. "I've heard it said that during the gold rush, new settlers often went *waltzing Matilda* from one gold find to another with their swags and shovels."

"Curiously, it is not used in New South Wales, to my knowledge," said Paterson. "I have not heard the expression before in my travels."

"Well, Barty," offered Bob, "as you know, much of Western Queensland has been taken up by people like ourselves from Victoria. So, maybe *waltzing Matilda* is used only in Victoria and Queensland."

"That might well be so, Bob," Barty agreed. "Christina, if we could be excused, would you mind playing for me on the autoharp again that tune which I liked so much?"

"Certainly, Barty. I shall be delighted, because I like it so much myself. Come on, everyone, let's go into the sitting room and we shall have some singing. You too, gentlemen. It's no good, Bob, taking them outside tonight with your demijohn full of rum and wild stories and good intentions!"

"Yes, come on," said Paterson, "but, before we all start singing, I want to see if we can have a new song. You see, I think *waltzing Matilda* fits to that lovely tune which Chris has been playing. I don't usually write songs, but she tells me that this music doesn't have any words and it has such a whimsical, dreamy melody that I believe it should have words to keep it alive. That's right, Chris, you still can't recall any words for it?"

"No, I can't, Barty. I heard it played by the

'Up came the squatter, a-riding his thoroughbred.'
Robert Curr, a renowned horseman of the North and present owner of Dagworth, mounted on his thoroughbred, Shambler, beside the grave of Bob Macpherson, squatter, and Jack Macpherson, overseer.

The site of old Dagworth, a short distance from graves on the main road.

One of the few remaining stumps of old Dagworth homestead.

band at the Warrnambool Steeplechase Meeting last April. I was there with my sister, Margaret, her husband, Stewart and their guests. I played the march when we returned to Meningoort that evening and one of the party suggested that it may once have been an old Scottish hymn. There are no words for it now that I know. This poor little autoharp won't do it justice. You should have heard it played by the Warrnambool band. It really was a masterpiece and it has such a strong, lilting melody that it is so easy to remember. Here it is again, Barty."

As the notes of Christina's memorised version of Craigielea tinkled from the little autoharp in that Victorian sitting room and wafted with an evening breeze through french doors towards the sleeping Diamantina and the world beyond, Barty Paterson played with words. "Once there was a swagman went waltzing Matilda...... no not quite .... Oh there once was a swagman camped in the billabong, under the shade of a coolibah tree .... that's it ... keep playing, Chris and we'll put in something about his billy and his tuckerbag and we'll put Bob in too!"

As Christina kept strumming the tune, Banjo's quick poetic mind provided more words ..... "Waltzing Matilda, Matilda, my darling, who'll come waltzing Matilda with me?"

Banjo soon had everyone singing one verse and a chorus. The rhyme scheme he was using was a very simple one and the complete verse, which he probably finished later that evening or next day, uses only five rhymes with four words: *tree, me, three,* and *glee.* Really, it is a very basic piece of work in structure and was no doubt finished in a very short space of time.

Much has since been written about how and where *Waltzing Matilda* came to be written and even Paterson's authorship was questioned. Significantly, this doubt was not expressed until after his death. Paterson was, we are assured, a man of great integrity and honesty and we can be quite certain that he was not writing a parody of an existing song, but writing fresh and original

'Notes wafted towards the sleeping Diamantina and the world beyond.'

words which related to recent personal experiences. He was to publish *Waltzing Matilda* as his own work as part of *Saltbush Bill, J.P. and Other Verses*, in 1917, and there are on record several statements which he made about writing the song. (See appendices G and H)

In the second of these, written in a letter to Mr Laurie Copping of Canberra dated 16th June, 1939, on Australian Club notepaper, Paterson stated that he wrote the song while travelling in Queensland and that he put words to a tune for which the lady who played it could not remember any. He referred to this person as being "afterwards Mrs McCowan". We know that this was, in fact, Christina's sister, Jean, who married Sam McCowan.

It is quite possible that Banjo's confusion, many years after the event, in his old age, may have been caused by a later development in the story. At the time Paterson wrote to Mr Copping, he was seventy-five and had only two years to live. Thirty-six years earlier, in 1903, he gave his approval to an arrangement of *Waltzing Matilda* by a Marie Cowan for use by tea merchants, Inglis and Company. The similarity in names makes one wonder whether he thought at the time he was dealing with Christina Macpherson, thinking she had married McCowan.

In the same letter, Paterson said that he did not think the verse had appeared in any of his books and that Mrs Paterson said it had not. This would seem to indicate that Banjo had no concern about challenges to his authorship, if he could not remember having published the verse in 1917.

In January, 1895, at Dagworth, nobody had any doubts about how the song which was to become world famous came to be. The Dagworth party was soon singing a new song with nothing special about it other than it was a bit of fun for a famous balladist and great entertainment for his friends.

We know that Paterson left a copy of his words at Dagworth and the permanent book-keeper, J. T. Wilson, found the song being sung there on his return from a long holiday in July. Significantly, Wilson said that the tune then being sung was similar to the popular one today except that it had been altered and he thought *not for the better in the second line*.

In retrospect, we must agree, for Christina's music is much more melodious and *whimsical* in the second line for the words *under the shade of a*

Graves of old Dagworth and the later Dagworth Hotel.

coolibah tree. It is a great pity that Marie Cowan, in 1903, changed or did not know these notes.

Paterson's stay at Dagworth coming to an end, he returned with his fiancée, Sarah, to Winton with others of the Dagworth party. Again, the night was spent at Ayrshire Downs with the Morrisons. Their daughter, Helen, was seven at the time and remembered the night for the rest of her life. In 1967, she told the author and wrote:

When they returned to Ayrshire Downs, 'Banjo' Paterson came into our nursery and read his new song to us children.

The party then returned to Winton and stayed with Mr Frederick Whistler Riley and his wife. That evening they sang 'Waltzing Matilda' to Christina's piano accompaniment.

Not long afterwards a banquet was held at the North Gregory Hotel and 'Waltzing Matilda' was sung in public by Herbert Ramsay, later Sir Herbert.

I had in my possession the toast list used at this

banquet, which I have since given to the Women's Historical Association of Queensland.

After returning South 'Banjo' Paterson wrote to both my mother and Mrs Riley, thanking them for their hospitality, and in my mother's letter he enclosed the original piece of paper they used for the words of 'Waltzing Matilda'. This was treasured in our home in my mother's life-time, but I regret to say it was lost after her death in 1937.

The reason why I have not made these statements public in the past is that I have always hoped the Manuscript would be found.

Helen Anderson.

The story of the Morrisons' copy of the song was the same everywhere. For years a search for an original manuscript went on throughout Australia and overseas. The answer was always the same with copies being lost or accidentally burned over the years during which *Waltzing Matilda* was quietly finding its way into the hearts of the Australian people.

The song was an instant hit in Winton. The Dagworth party made first for *Aloha* in Vindex Street, the home of Sarah's brother, Frederick Riley, and his new wife, Marie. Here they made straight for the piano, while Marie made afternoon tea.

Half a century later, Mrs Riley recalled the events of that afternoon for Sydney May when he was researching material for his book, *The Story of Waltzing Matilda*. May wrote:

Arriving in Winton, the party was joined by Herbert Ramsay, the possessor of a good baritone voice, who accompanied them to Mrs Riley's home. No afternoon tea for them — there was a piano and the new song must be sung right away. Vainly, Mrs Riley called to them that the tea was getting cold. They kept on trying, over and over again, and so Waltzing Matilda assumed shape. Two separate people, both still living, affirm that the music was definitely set down on paper, but it was never published or copyrighted.

It has always been accepted in Winton that, following the afternoon tea party, everyone went on to the North Gregory Hotel. Mrs Riley's home was not a large one, as may be seen from the foundations remaining on a vacant block of land. It certainly would not have accommodated all of the visitors, so probably some stayed at the North Gregory. The song was sung at the hotel that night.

Dagworth horses, 1980, sketched by **Susie Whitcombe**, a world-renowned painter of horses.

The Manuscript

After a few days in Winton, Paterson set off on the long journey to Sydney and his legal practice in the firm, Street and Paterson. After a coach trip to Longreach, he travelled to Rockhampton, where he boarded the steamer *S.S. Burwah*. He disembarked in Brisbane on 7th February, leaving for Sydney by train on the 9th.

At home, Paterson began polishing the manuscript of his first book, *The Man from Snowy River and Other Verses*. This was to be published in October that year by Angus and Robertson. Following its release and immediate popularity, *The Banjo* made another visit to Winton, partly to escape the publicity, which he always disliked, and mainly to see his fiancée again. During this visit, Paterson went to see a bushfire-fighting demonstration at Oondooroo Station, owned by the Ramsay brothers. It was Herbert Ramsay who sang *Waltzing Matilda* when it was first played in Winton and the song was again sung during Paterson's visit to Oondooroo.

Meanwhile, Herbert Ramsay had already made the song well known and popular in the Winton district. It was already being taken up by the shearers and station workers. Drovers also were singing the song around their campfires and spreading it wide across the inland.

It seems that the shearers, defeated by the squatters in the previous year's bitter struggle, saw the swagman as their martyr. Accordingly, they changed Paterson's line, *Drowning himself by the coolabah tree* to the more defiant "*You'll never take me alive,*" said he.

On the other end of the social spectrum, Herbert Ramsay had rendered *Waltzing Matilda* for the Premier of Queensland, Mr Hugh Nelson, during a banquet in his honour at Winton. The Premier visited the town to receive deputations calling for the construction of a railway to the town. This banquet was held on 6th April, 1895. The catchy and provocative bush song from Dagworth would be heard by many more important people at many grand occasions far into the

Mrs Curr always has plenty of company at Dagworth despite the isolation. The homestead in which our song was written was moved here in 1898 and these rooms are located under the high hip roof on the right.

'The races brought everyone to town.' Nelia Racecourse

future. This was not to be known by those who lived around the genesis of the song in those distant days. Many copies of it were made, later to lose their curiosity value and disappear from sight and memory. Fortunately, there was to be one exception.

The Winton Races, postponed because of rain from 24th and 25th May, 1895, were held on the 28th and 29th of that month. This race meeting was a great occasion in those days, the equivalent of annual festivals held by many towns today. The races and associated social functions brought everybody in the district to town and many visitors from far afield.

Waltzing Matilda was sung many times during the race festival and was afterwards to be taken yet further and wider through the Australian bush. One of those who heard the song then for the first time was Mr W. B. Bartlam, a stock and station agent from Townsville. Mr Bartlam had managed properties in the Hughenden-Winton district for some years before moving to Townsville to found a pastoral agency which was financed by many of the Western pastoralists whose interests Mr Bartlam would care for at the sea port. So, his visit to the Winton Races would have been something of a public relations exercise as well as allowing an opportunity for him and his wife to renew old friendships. The Bartlams and Macpherson were friends of old.

During that race festival, Christina Macpherson wrote out and gave to Mr Bartlam or his wife the words and music of *Waltzing Matilda*. A photograph of this manuscript, which came to the author from Mr Bartlam's son in Hobart is reproduced here. It is surely significant that this prize was to come back to where it was written from the other end of Australia after seventy-six years.

The manuscript's authenticity is unquestionably established. The handwriting matches samples of Christina's writing from the same period supplied by her niece, Mrs Islay McIntosh, of Melbourne. The owner of the manuscript, Mr J. R. Y. Bartlam, (son of W.B.) had his daughter, Barbara, take it to the Tasmanian State Library to have it examined for the author in 1971. There, the Chief Archivist recorded that the paper was machine made, with no water mark and was of a type common from about 1880. It was written in

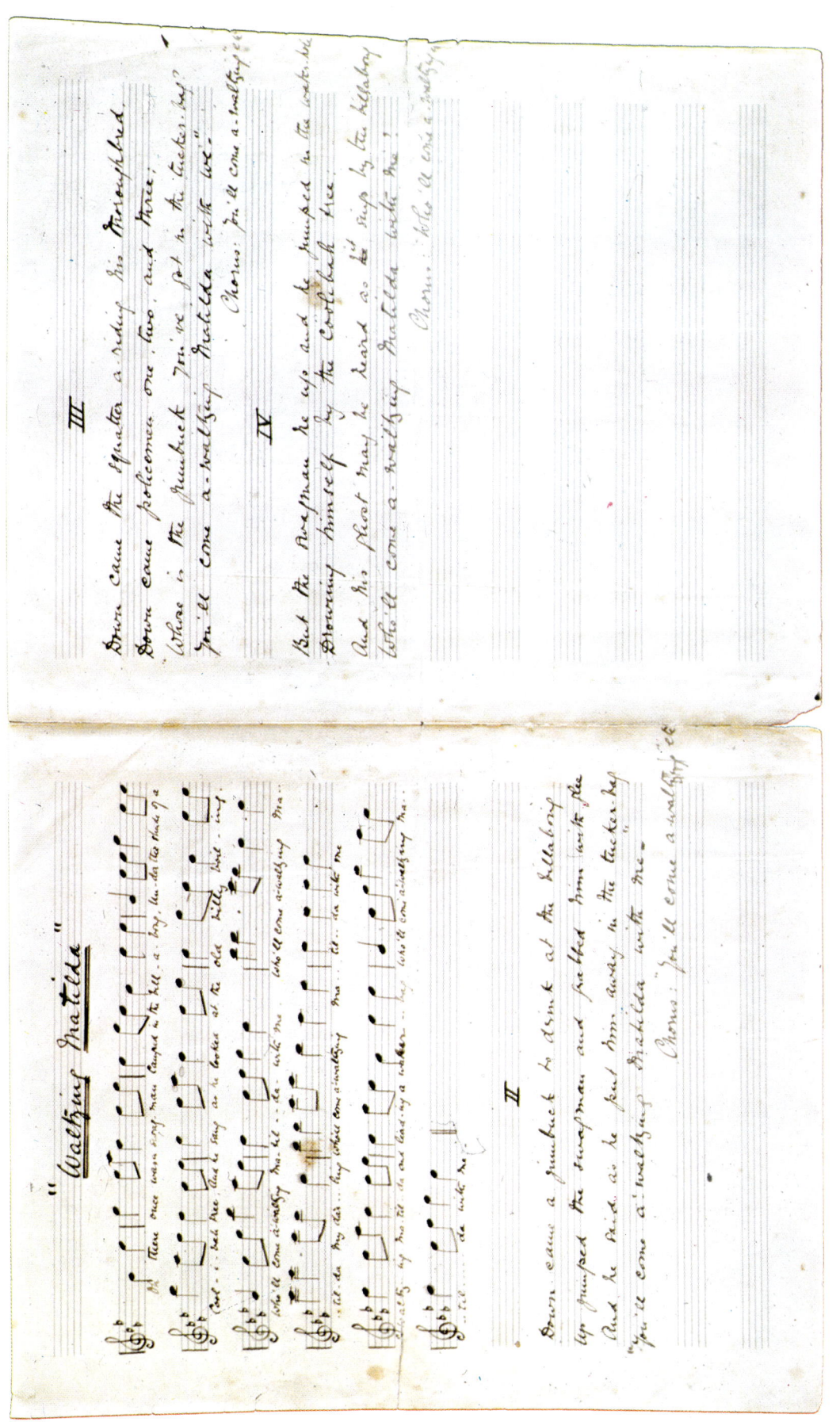

The original *Waltzing Matilda*, in Christina Macpherson's own hand. This manuscript was given to Mr and Mrs W. B. Bartlam at the Winton Race Carnival, May, 1895. It is now held by their grand-daughter in Hobart, Tasmania. An arrangement of this music, as the author believes Christina meant it to be sung, may be found in the appendix.

ordinary nineteenth century ink with a steel type nib common at that time. The writing is typical of a well educated lady of 1835 onwards to early 1900 and a 'very usual' writing of that period.

More important is the fact that Mrs McIntosh was certain the writing was that of her aunt. On 23rd December, 1971, she wrote:

Thank you for your interesting letter and for that wonderful treasure — the copy of Aunt Chris's Waltzing Matilda.

The minute I opened it out, her so familiar writing leaped out at me, as though she was there and writing it for us. Her writing was just as familiar to me as that of my parents. Aunt Chris was my first governess — the first of many, because we lived mostly in the country and I never went to school.

Despite the Christmas rush, I have already begun to search through old papers to find a note or letter or something to verify it with and I hope to be successful, though it might take me a week or two. She died so long ago, somewhere in the Thirties, and she had few possessions then. She always signed herself "Chris", or "C.R.", or "C.R.M." — never Christina.

I am confident something will turn up, perhaps on a photograph or on the fly leaf of a book.

Fortunately, the search paid dividends and Mrs McIntosh was able to provide a number of excellent samples of Christina's handwriting which covered a considerable period of her life. There are two from the time when she wrote her *Waltzing Matilda* manuscript which appear to have been written with the same pen and ink.

The presence of W. B. Bartlam at the Winton races is also a matter of history. A Brisbane newspaper, *The Queenslander*, of 8th June, 1895, gives a detailed report of the racing and concludes with this paragraph:

The starting machine fully performed all that could be expected, and everyone was loud in its praise. The visitors were numerous, numbering, besides those from the country, Messrs L. Goldring and P. Gannon from Hughenden, and Mr W. B. Bartlam from Townsville.

So, the chain of events which began centuries ago is complete with regard to the origins of our song.

We have the *old Scottish hymn* and its related band march, *Craigielee*, and we have seen that this was played at the Warrnambool races in April, 1894. We now also have Christina Macpherson's adaptation of that march which became *Waltzing Matilda* the following January. Furthermore, we know the background of events from which Paterson was able to draft his ballad.

Each link of this chain has been forged by solid documentary and historical evidence, so that Australians today can be quite certain about the origins of their national song and know that it is a true ballad and a product of the Australian bush.

Matilda, that footloose woman of ill repute, has risen far above her former station in life to be company fit for kings and princes, presidents and potentates, even prime-ministers and premiers! Albeit unwittingly, she has become the legendary heroine of a defacto National Anthem.

Matilda may never have any formal or legal bond with her adopted country, nevertheless, in the hearts of her own people and in the eyes of the world at large, she and Australia are inseparable.

At Winton, it soon became an established practice for the town's own song to be presented at official occasions and celebrations. It is recorded that Herbert Ramsay again rendered Winton's "hit" at banquets on 25th July, 1899, and 13th June, 1907.

A. B. Paterson made another visit to Winton early in 1896. He certainly did a lot of travelling. Absence makes the heart grow fonder and romance in the bush can shorten distances by many miles. However, it seems that this was to be the Banjo's last visit to the district, because, at this time, or soon afterwards, his engagement to Sarah Riley was broken. We know that the now famous poet travelled by train to Rockhampton with Inspector Lamond and his family, arriving in that city on 13th March. The Lamonds there boarded a ship which would take them to Cooktown and we also know that their luggage was lost between the train and the ship, so that they went on without it. Despite the isolation and privations of those pioneering days, it is truly remarkable how many detailed records have been preserved in Queensland.

The little outback town of Winton not only gave us our national song, it gave us our international airline, *Qantas*. The company, *Queensland and Northern Territory Aerial Services*, was founded there in 1920.

Just as the fledgling airline was to spread its wings and fly further and further across Australia and then the world, so it was with *Matilda*.

The Cities and Towns

The song was first sung on foreign soil during the Boer War in South Africa. Many Western Queensland horsemen served in this campaign, including several from the Winton district. One of these later recalled having joined in singing *Waltzing Matilda* in the South African bush. There were numerous reports also of the song being sung by troops returning to Sydney.

Many more thousands of soldiers would later sing of a swagman and a billabong while going to and from other wars, but these Boer War veterans were responsible for making the song known in Sydney. There, an enterprising tea merchant, James Inglis, quickly recognised the song's potential as a singing commercial for his product. He was soon making enquiries with the aim of securing rights to use this piece about a bushman waiting for his billy to boil, to brew his tea.

Meanwhile, back in the bush, hard times had befallen the pioneers of North West Queensland. Kings in grass castles they surely were, for a long, withering drought destroyed those castles and brought many squatters low. Like the swagmen, some of these men now found themselves broke to the world and on the move, seeking employment. One of these was Bob Macpherson.

Bob, with only his swag and his buckboard, moved to the Cloncurry district, where he found a position as manager of Coolulah Station. Bob never married, but about 1898, in Winton, he began an affair with Josephine Pene, a dressmaker and pianist, piano teacher. Josephine had previously been engaged to the Honourable Francis Hay, of Needlewood Station, Muttaburra. Hay committed suicide earlier in 1898.

Josephine bore a son to Bob Macpherson on 17th September, 1900. Bob refused to marry and, in retaliation, Josephine had the child registered and baptised as Dagworth Robert Rutherford Macpherson Pene. She later filed a paternity suit and, while the result of this is not known, nor has it been researched, it is known that Bob supported Josephine and the boy for many years.

The author has met and spent some time with Bob Macpherson's son and grandson, so this part of our story comes direct from them.

Not long after Bob Macpherson moved to Cloncurry, he provided a home for Josephine and the boy in that town and spent much of his time with them. Josephine had her piano and continued to take pupils. Bob often joined her at the piano and their son fondly recalls many happy songs which they sang. One of these was a variant of the *Waltzing Matilda* tune which Dagworth was to remember always as his mother's favourite. He revealed this during an interview in 1971, during which this tune was played. This music was first collected and published by ballad authority, John Manifold as the *Queensland Version*, or *Buderim Tune*.

It is significant that this tune has always been known in the author's family as the *Cloncurry Version* and the author was born in Cloncurry. In view of the foregoing evidence, it appears that the Macpherson family has links with both Matilda tunes and that Josephine Pene should be credited with the lovely tune which makes the Queensland or Cloncurry Version such a delightfully captivating folksong.

As the song spread through the bush with itinerant shearers, drovers, cooks and station hands, words and tune took on numerous variations. In fact, even today, while the tune may be universal, one seldom hears two people sing the same words!

Matilda came quietly into most towns and stayed. Nobody asked questions about her past or her antecedents. Such questions were not asked, because there were many remittance men in the bush whose earlier lives remained a respected mystery. So it was that most strangers in towns far from Winton assumed Matilda had been in the bush a long time and left it at that.

This was not so in Hughenden, to the North of Winton. Matilda was given a rousing, riotous reception there in 1902 by the *Greenhide Gang*.

'The Sphinx' guards Cloncurry's Eastern approaches

'Bob, with only his swag and his buckboard, moved to the Cloncurry district.'

After the Second World War, an article entitled *How "Waltzing Matilda" Came to Hughenden* appeared in *The North Australian Monthly*. It was written by F. P. Archer, then resident in Rabaul, New Britain. Fred Archer spent his early life in Western Queensland and, when ten years old, he saw and heard Matilda come to Hughenden. Here is his lively account:

In April, 1902, a bush song came to Hughenden and neither before nor since has any song created such a sensation. It was race time and naturally everybody for miles around was in town: squatters, ringers, shearers, kangaroo shooters, carriers, bush-workers, and visitors from as far as Charters Towers, then at its peak and capital of the North.

The 'Greenhide Push', all young bloods, organised a procession up the main street, Brodie Street, four abreast, made up of young station men, stockmen and blackboys. There were F. W. Riley on his grey horse from Winton, Bob and Gideon Macpherson of Dagworth, Mayor Blackall of Hughenden, T. Jillett of Cassilis, head of the Greenhides. They got the Salvation Army's big drum, some cornets and tambourines and the black boys, gum leaves. The streets were crowded with people. The drum boomed, wild notes came from the cornets, tambourines clashed — all in the theme song, 'Waltzing Matilda'.

The crowds on the footpath took it up, horses started to buck and throw their riders, the black boys thumbed their mounts and beat them with their wide-brimmed hats. They yelled and so did everyone else. The drummer was down but couldn't care less, he still continued whacking the drum — boom-boom. Bucking horses were everywhere. Finally, the procession reached the Great Western-Hughenden Hotels and such horses as were under control were tied to hitching posts.

Tall, lean men in white Canton riding trousers, red shirts, riding boots and long-necked spurs were among the crowds that milled through the hotels, thumped the pianos, roared 'Waltzing Matilda' from beginning to end, over and over again, in parlour, bar and verandah, while excited horsemen rode into the middle of the singers and took up the chorus. Dan Wright, a tobacconist, and a former Imperial Army soldier, seized a bugle from a nail in his shop and was in the crowd blowing Reveille. The Charge, The Retreat, Boots and Saddle, Cookhouse, everything he could think of. He kept on even after he was well lit up, and though spreadeagled in the gutter, still blew army calls.

This carried on for several hours on the first day till all were exhausted.

Next day the Greenhides got a bullocky to hitch up his team, and, with the whole Salvation Army Band on the wagon, went playing 'Waltzing Matilda' at every place they could think of. Towards evening a crowd of mounted men, kangaroo shooters and others, rode down Brodie Street. They galloped through the crowd with rifles and revolvers blazing in the air, punctuating the bellowed words of the song. This they kept up till they reached the police station, yelled out for troopers 1,2,3, then laid whips to their horses and bolted over Havelock Park to the west, out of town to escape the rising wrath of the law. And so was 'Waltzing Matilda' launched in N.W. Queensland before any Australian cities even heard of it.'

Fred Archer, an elderly man possessed of an excellent memory and literary craftsmanship, provided much more interesting information for the author in a number of letters written during the late Sixties:

I think the 'Official Pianist' for the Greenhides — who played in the Hughenden Hotel parlor — was a selector from Tower Hill Creek named Davis, who kept the music going and had drinks lined up on top of the piano ready for consumption during intervals. Both George Robinson and Ben Howell 'had been on the Palmer' and rose nobly to this occasion and made all the boys welcome. I met Davis — then called 'Dad' Davis, again in New Guinea — he died of fever in Madang. The song had been sung by bushmen round 'the Gulf Country' for some time before this Hughenden sing-song and it just so happened that it was the most popular song at the time and so was chosen as the premier item for the occasion. It being Boer War time, there were various patriotic songs about — 'Sons of the Sea', 'Soldiers of the Queen', etc. In all of these songs they repeated the chorus faithfully after each verse.

Now in Waltzing Matilda — as I have set it down — it just swung along without any high-faluting stuff, about 'jolly jumbucks' and 'Troopers' instead of policemen, and in some versions the squatter was 'mounted on his thoroughbred' but he was just riding it as we used to sing it. After each verse we sang the chorus with a slight variation each time to follow as it were,

Hills at Carisbrook, Winton.

'They laid whips to their horses and bolted West from the wrath of the law.'

'A Cairns for me and a Fourex for m' horse.'

the events narrated in the previous chapter — but we certainly did that always — in bush land in those times.

You mention the papers — setting out the song — that were on the walls of the hotels. Well, the 'Hughenden Observer' of those days was owned by various station people and local businessmen and they (the paper) used to print 'dodgers' concerning news that came through, between issues, and distributed them round town — they were usually posted in hotels too — I do recall that the Editor — a large man named Wheeler — had some of these dodgers done with 'Waltzing Matilda' set out — and these were distributed and so what your friend mentioned came from that source. When the compositor got too drunk, on an important occasion, these papers were awfully smudged and sometimes back to front printing — but no one was greatly worried.

The other informant who had referred to the leaflets was Gilbert Weale, of Townsville, who remembered learning the words of Waltzing Matilda from the walls of Hughenden hotels:

The leadflet, as I remember it, was about eight inches by five inches. I am not quite sure who was the printer, but I have an idea it was the Hughenden paper, the editor of which was a man named Wheeler. I never saw any music, but the tune was very popular, and I learnt it from hearing it sung so often by the men in the pubs, and by Mrs James Penny, daughter-in-law of Tom Penny, the butcher, and by Mrs Alexander of Caithness Station.

So, here we have evidence from two living witnesses that the words of Waltzing Matilda were first printed in Hughenden, in 1902, beating Sydney to the punch by just one year.

Fred Archer and Gilbert Weale provided almost identical copies of the words and, significantly, both used the phrase through the billabong — a unique variation. Otherwise, their texts followed Paterson's very closely. This is not

'Excited horsemen rode in and took up the chorus.'

surprising, because Fred Archer named the Macpherson brothers and Fred Riley as members of the rip-roaring *Greenhide Gang*. No doubt, Editor Wheeler obtained the words of the song directly from them.

Fred Archer was to add more colour to various aspects of our story:

I don't remember anything about a shearer being shot in 1894 at Dagworth. I suppose that might have been during the '94 strike. At that time most of the squatters thought all shearers ought to be shot.

I remember the Quinlan family lived in Hughenden and that the father was a boundary rider at Dagworth, but I only saw him on one or two occasions. People said he preferred to keep to himself.

I knew Bob Macpherson as owner of Dagworth, and a good fellow and great host and being 'well into the bank' — he was good to us kids when he came across us anywhere. My father was on Round Hill station in his teens, near Albury, and the place where Dan Morgan seemed to haunt. There were shepherds there who were 'old lags' from Tasmania and they kept Morgan well supplied with information and mutton. They all hated the squatters of course. My Dad reckoned he was 'the most cold blooded scoundrel Australia has produced who shot men in their sleep'. (Our more modern gents can equal him though.)

One thing more — I notice you ask about the tune that went with Waltzing Matilda in the early days; well, I should say it is the same now as then.

It is an important fact that all of the old-timers, who learnt the tune in its early days in the bush, record that the tune then was essentially the same as the popular version today. So, any arguments which support other composers are simply academic pipe dreaming or drum beating.

For example, the music firm Allan and Company, Sydney, for many years continued to beat a drum for Marie Cowan as composer. They, of course, had their own good commercial reasons for this.

As mentioned earlier, the tea merchant, James Inglis, saw the song's potential as a singing commercial for his Billy Tea, the packets of which depicted a bushman boiling his billy.

Allans say that Inglis bought the advertising rights from Angus and Robertson, but the publishers have never been able to find any record of this and suggested that Inglis may have dealt directly with Paterson, although he had sold the verse with an assortment of other pieces to Angus and Robertson for five pounds.

Anyway, it is a matter of history that James Inglis secured permission to use the song and asked Marie Cowan, the wife of his manager, to write an arrangement. It is said that Paterson telephoned or wired to compliment her on the finished product. It is here that the similarity of the names Cowan and McCowan holds interest.

That Marie Cowan's melody is so little different from the Macpherson music is not surprising, for the Boer War veterans and others had brought the song to Sydney. Also, if Marie Cowan had contact with Paterson, then it is most likely he would have given her the existing tune as well as the words.

Several noteworthy alterations were made to the text. The swagman became *jollified* in the opening line, no doubt in anticipation of enjoying his *Billy Tea*. Likewise, *leading a waterbag* was removed from the chorus, so that *Billy*, with a capital B, could be repeated. However, the most regrettable alteration was that made to the tune in the second line where the note is repeated. It was here that the song lost so much of the *whimsicality* which first captivated Paterson.

When Inglis printed the song, words were attributed to Paterson and Marie Cowan was shown to be merely the arranger. It is said that Mrs Cowan wanted nothing to do with royalties when she discovered that her work was to be used for advertising purposes, so that proceeds due to her were paid to charity.

Allans later bought rights to the music and when Mrs Cowan died, her husband, Russell Cowan gave them a statement to the effect that his wife had indeed been the composer. The disposition of royalties since that time has remained confidential.

The Inglis publication certainly served to spread the song much more quickly. Copies were circulated amongst the troops during the First World War and there are several reports of the song having been sung at the front. The poem, *Singing Soldiers*, by C. J. Dennis, records use of *Waltzing Matilda* at Gallipoli, in 1915.

Whether you're sitting on a bucking bull, a campdrafting horse, or just on a fence, there's plenty of excitement at the rodeo.

The annual rodeo brings festival time in the Waltzing Matilda country

When announcements have all been made, and prizes presented to the sun-bronzed champions, those who came just for the fun can always find a couple of clowns to share a cold Fourex, Queensland's popular beer.

The World

The Jolly Swagman statue, Winton, Queensland

'Just as the fledgling airline was to spread its wings and fly further and further across Australia and then the world, so it was with Matilda.'

'WALTZING MATILDA'

 OFFICIAL WESLEY FIRST DAY COVER

Soon, the song would be appearing in many forms. In 1918, the words were printed in a songbook for Australian troops, being taken from an earlier publication, *The Australian Students' Song Book*. This was released in 1911 and had a wide circulation.

The man who did most for the popularisation of *Waltzing Matilda* in the years before the Second World War was Thomas Wood. He travelled in Australia as an examiner for The Royal Schools of Music and afterwards published a book, *Cobbers*, which proved immensely popular, going through several editions. Each of these editions contained the words and music of *Waltzing Matilda* as published by Allan and Company in 1930. Allans had bought the rights to the words from Angus and Robertson for three guineas, although the publishers retained the right to print them in future editions of Paterson's collected verse.

Now there came a dispute between Allans and Thomas Wood's publishers, Oxford University Press. This was eventually settled amicably enough, with future editions showing Marie Cowan as the composer and Wood as the arranger.

Thomas Wood got his story about the origins of the song in Winton from Mr Tom Shanahan, then licensee of the North Gregory Hotel. Shanahan had his version of events from Jack Lawton who was horsebreaker at Dagworth when the song was written. It was Lawton's own belief that he saw and heard the song composed during the journey from Dagworth to Winton at the end of Paterson's stay. Lawton certainly did accompany the party as spareboy, that is, he was in charge of the spare horses for the station drag.

No doubt, the song was sung during the journey. It is believed locally that it was sung at the Dick's Creek Hotel. Lawton, however, would not necessarily have known that the song had been composed earlier at Dagworth, because the horsebreaker was an *outside* man and would not have had any social intercourse with members of the house party. There was a distinct dividing line drawn in those days and for many years afterwards between the two main social classes in the bush — those *inside* and those *outside*. This referred particularly to where people took their meals. Until comparatively recent times, there were still country towns where a line was drawn down the centre of dance floors. This was known as the Chalk Line.

To digress for a moment, it is interesting to note that at the time Christina Macpherson wrote the music of *Waltzing Matilda*, it was not acceptable for young ladies of society to publish music. This may explain her failure to make any claim, as well as Paterson's reticence on the subject.

Despite Thomas Wood's use of Lawton's

'A song which made them easily identified as Australians.'

erroneous story, his publication of words and music certainly made the song widely known in Australia and the British Isles. *Cobbers* was first published in 1934.

During the Second World War, the song of the billabongs was taken still further across the world, wherever Australian diggers went. It was a song which easily evoked memories of home and made them easily identified as Australians.

While *Advance Australia Fair* was gaining great mileage at home, being played by the A.B.C. to introduce news bulletins, Matilda was making acquaintances in faraway lands whence she herself had come.

Soldiers of other allied nations learnt the song from Australians and these included thousands of Americans who were stationed in this country during the latter part of the War. Of course, many of these men not only took Matilda home with them, but an Aussie war bride too.

A recording of *Waltzing Matilda* made during the war by the great Australian bass baritone, Peter Dawson, also contributed to the song's growing acceptance and popularity. Some years later, Harry Belafonte was to make a recording which took Matilda into every American home, winning many more friends there for a lonely swagman from the land *Down Under*.

Millions of Americans and people of many other nations came to know Australia's song much better after seeing the popular film *On the Beach* which was made from the novel by Australian writer, Nevil Shute. *Waltzing Matilda* featured prominently in the film and producer, Kramer, had this to say: *This is a remarkably versatile song. It can be played as a folk tune, a march, a ballad or in any other musical form, and we have used it in a dozen different ways in the score for "On the Beach". I decided, almost on the spur of the moment, that "Waltzing Matilda" should be the feature tune of the film's musical score.*

One of Matilda's greatest moments came during the closing ceremony for the 1956 Olympic Games in Melbourne. A massed choir took Australia's own song to the world from a huge stadium in a great city not far from where Matilda first set foot in Australia. It was only a short distance too from the country race track where a girl from Melbourne once heard that

Sydney Cove, Port Jackson, site of the First Fleet's landing, 26th January, 1788.

provocative march, Craigielee, sixty-two years earlier.

In another huge stadium, during the Twelfth Commonwealth Games at Brisbane, in September, 1982, Matilda won the hearts of millions of people across the globe in the guise of a giant kangaroo which waltzed imperially around the arena, pausing to wink at royalty and thousands of cheering fans.

For the last words about *Waltzing Matilda's* journey from a lonely pioneer homestead and a small outback colonial town to the capitals of the world, let us return to the story of Allan and Company, music publishers:

Mr Inglis died in 1908 and the song received little attention until after the outbreak of war in 1914, when copies were distributed among military camps and the song began to take on. When Mrs Cowan died in 1919, Waltzing Matilda had already entered on a new era boosted by the voices of returning servicemen. In 1925 Inglis & Co's rights in the song having automatically become vested in the estate of Marie Cowan, all publishing rights were assigned to Allan & Co. Pty Ltd. on an agreement of equal division of any profits. The estate's share of the profits was to be devoted to charity and since then several charities have benefited substantially.

It is interesting to note that 'Waltzing Matilda' has been assigned to and published in, the following countries: U.S.A., Canada, Mexico, United Kingdom, France, Belgium, Switzerland, Luxemburg, Germany, Austria, Italy, Denmark, Norway, Sweden, Finland, Spain, Portugal, Netherlands, Israel, Japan and all countries of Central and South America.

It does seem a pity that those who composed a song which has made so much money got so little from it. Christina Macpherson died in 1936 in poor circumstances, having received no money and little recognition. When Paterson died, in 1941, he left an estate of a little over £200. However, he was able to enjoy the success of his own literary work in his own lifetime, including the popularity of *Waltzing Matilda*. Once, in Sydney, he heard and saw soldiers singing and marching to his song, prior to their departure for the First World War. He said to his friend, Daryl Lindsay, "Well, Daryl, I only got a fiver for the song, but it's worth a million to me to hear it sung like that!" At least Christina would have shared this pleasure.

'Who'll come a-waltzing Matilda, my darling?'

The Combined Military Forces Band. Matilda welcomed the world to the Commonwealth Games.

'You'll never take me alive! said he.'

Shearers, taking the swagman as their martyr changed the line, 'Drowning himself by the coolibah tree'.

'You'll come a-waltzing Matilda with me!'

Aussie medal winners came to the victory dais at the Commonwealth Games, 'Waltzing Matilda'.

 # The Ghost

Will *Waltzing Matilda* ever become Australia's National Anthem? What does it matter? We seem to have two already, one of them an outdated hymn with arthritic words, while the words of the other — well, who knows them anyway?

All that aside, is Waltzing Matilda made of the stuff from which national anthems are forged? Is it a song of social significance?

At the end of chapter five, the reader was asked several questions and should now be better placed to answer the last two:

Is Waltzing Matilda just a frivolous ballad, or is it an allegory? Is the song symbolic of great social conflict which we have chosen to forget, but which the ghost of a swagman calls us to remember?

To assist the reader with a verdict, two witnesses will now be called. To put the negative opinion, here is Oscar Mendelsohn, of Melbourne, with extracts from his book, *A Waltz with Matilda* (1966):

The song has never been associated with any economic struggle, social upheaval, national or patriotic movement. Indeed, it has never stood for anything specific whatever. It has been accepted as a vague Australian symbol of nationality, but beyond this it is impossible to discover any clear-cut path or trend. (p. 13)

Here we have no suggestion of outlawry or of the good poor fighting the bad rich. The unnamed swagman is not discernably any sort of a hero and there is no suggestion of war against brutal police. Here is merely a simple jingling story of a swagman caught stealing a sheep. There are no ethical or political implications either way.

The conclusion is clear, at any rate to me, that "Waltzing Matilda" has never been in any sense a song of social significance, and for what it is worth, I put on record the opinion that it is unlikely that it will ever become one. The song has lived and grown by a tuneful melody grafted on to a naive story embellished with a quaint and obscure phrase or two. (pp. 15-16)

"The Star Spangled Banner" is a good specimen of a rallying song whose theme transcends sound judgement. . . . . . The author of the words of "The Star Spangled Banner" was Francis Scott Key (1799-1843), who wrote them in 1814 after witnessing the defence of Fort McHenry against the British bombardment. . . . . . "The commander of the British ship should have been court-martialled for wasting powder on such a stupid action. The United States has had plenty of heroic deeds in her history worthy of commemoration without picking this silly episode." (p. 11)

Another song of particular interest is "John Brown's Body". Once again the tune is an old one (a hymn, "Say, brothers, will you meet us?"), and the words are the important element. The song, commencing "John Brown's body lies a-mouldering in the grave, but his soul goes marching on", quickly became a favourite of the Northern Army in the American Civil War. The "John Brown" grew to be recognized as the hero of Harper's Ferry and the words acquired a political meaning.

The John Brown of Harper's Ferry was a fantastic character, best remembered as a violent opponent of slavery. He believed any means were justified to stamp it out. He was hanged at Charleston in 1859. According to Professor Osborne (and at the age of ninety-two his memory remains almost incredibly acute): "The actual John Brown of the American Civil War was a homicidal monomaniac who deserved the mental hospital and not the gallows. He instructed his sons and followers to kill every slave-owner and then to open the chest and examine the heart to see if it was all right with the Lord."

Observe that here a song becomes identified by the accident of name with a person of doubtful heroic stature, and that the same song then becomes a focal point for many turbulent movements. Of course, the tune is a superb marching melody. How does the reader rank the tune of "Waltzing Matilda" against "John Brown's Body" as a march? (p. 12)

To put the affirmative stance that *Waltzing Matilda* is indeed a song of social significance, we have a lengthy but provocative statement from a witness whose evidence the author found in the Mitchell Library. This was an article written in the United States for "The Yale Review" by William Power, in 1954:

"Waltzing Matilda" could, if distorted, be interpreted as a social protest along Marxist lines. If it were merely a protest, it would hardly have been accepted as a national rallying song at a time when Australians felt they were fighting for their national existence. It is a song of affirmation.

Australians believe that they have achieved an unusually good life for the average citizen. By a good life, they would understand not only the material necessities, but an opportunity for the human spirit to develop. These conditions have not been achieved without effort. Australians have had to struggle not only with the forces of nature, but with the short-comings of human nature. Within the Australian society there have been many conflicts political, and economic, and they were not resolved without bitterness and injustice. The fact remains that the average Australian is proud of what his country has accomplished.

These tensions find expression in 'Waltzing Matilda', the antagonists being the two extreme types, squatter and swagman. In such a conflict, most would declare that the squatter deserves to win. The economy of Australia depends largely on his prowess as a sheep or cattle raiser. He is hard-working, responsible, daring; if he lacked any of

'Whose is the jumbuck?'

Tar-branding sheep

the qualities which we associate with the pioneer, he would not remain a squatter for long. By almost any test, he is a more valuable citizen than the swagman.

But the squatter did not achieve his success without trampling on some human rights. The swagman, too, is a human being. Compared with the squatter, he may be shiftless; but he cannot be ignored. He, too, is part of society. Some few swagmen rose to become squatters; more achieved a lesser but still satisfactory status as farmers, station hands, mechanics, city workers; others remained landless and homeless to the end of their days, leaving their bones along the inland tracks. Society may require that the squatter shall prevail over the swagman, but the rights of the swagman as a human being must never be forgotten. If he has rights, he also has a contribution to make. Society must encourage the economic and civic virtues, but must also try to preserve the individualism of the wanderer, whose sturdy

anarchy will always have a potential value. If society is involved in an internal struggle, so is the individual. The spirit of the swagman must survive not only in society but in every man.

What has been said up to this point might apply to dealings between squatter and swagman at any point from, say, 1860 to 1935. (In the twentieth century the detail of the troopers' caps would have to be modified.) But 'Waltzing Matilda' was written in a definite year, 1895, and the date is significant.

The first years of the 1890's were, in Australia, marked by great social upheavals. The country came closer than ever before or since to dividing along class lines. The labor unions were by 1890 well established, and embraced many rural workers. In a country with a population not much over a million and a half, the shearers' unions numbered some forty thousand members. (The shearers are highly skilled workers who travel from sheep station to sheep station.) Between 1890 and 1895 there was a series of strikes in both city and country. The two shearers' strikes of 1890 and 1894 were potentially the most explosive, especially as the shearers were bushmen accustomed to the use of arms and had declared their readiness to use them. The squatters were equally determined and, if they were outnumbered, they were able to call not only on the police but on the military. All the strikes were defeated, and the shearers in particular were put down hard. Squatter and shearer may well stand for the extremes of the two factions.

The defeat of the unions had a result that no one had foreseen. Observing that the employers had all governmental agencies, including the army, on their side, the labor leaders determined to gain control of the government — by peaceful means. Accordingly, the labor parties were formed, and the unions entered politics directly. In the twentieth century they have played a decisive part in Australian affairs, having been elected to office more often than the conservative parties. All this seems to have stemmed mainly from the failure of the strikes. The year 1895 may be regarded as a turning point in Australian history.

In 1895, however, what Paterson must have been chiefly conscious of was that the shearers had suffered a resounding defeat. He could hardly have avoided being conscious of this. 'Waltzing Matilda' was written at Dagworth, a sheep station

'The shearers were put down hard — a resounding defeat, and a turning point in Australian History.'

in Queensland. This was in the heart of the country which strikers and squatters had contested. Just a few months before Paterson wrote his poem, the woolsheds at Dagworth were burned by the strikers.

What was Paterson's attitude towards the strikers? He was by birth and upbringing a member of a squatting family. His verse, in general, sees life from the point of view of the squatter. On several occasions he engaged in controversy with his fellow poet, Henry Lawson, who stoutly upheld the working-class movement, and in 1890 actually wrote songs for the strikers. And Paterson was, when he wrote the poem, the guest of a squatter whose woolsheds had been sabotaged.

On the other hand, his verse never upholds oppression by the squatters. It shows a strong sympathy for the underdog, especially the bushworker. Henry Lawson and others accused him of idealizing the bushworker; it is possible that he tended to see bushmen, both squatters and shearers, as better than they actually were. It can hardly be doubted that in a showdown he would have sided with the squatters, but it is equally certain that he never lost sympathy for the shearers.

'Waltzing Matilda' does not tell us anything of the swagman's past. There was in 1895, however, an excellent chance that any swagman might be one of the defeated shearers out of work, with a grudge not only against squatters, but against society in general. The swagman, it must be noted, is formidable. The squatter calls on three troopers to arrest one man. This is not without its irony, and may reflect the fact that during the strikes the military forces called out by the squatters were overwhelming.

**Sunset at Birdsville,
'Heartbreak Corner', Queensland.**

How much of this historical background would the average Australian be familiar with? He would not, probably, know that Paterson wrote 'Waltzing Matilda' at Dagworth a few months after the strikers burned the woolsheds. He would, however, know of the strikes of the Nineties, the defeat of the strikers, the growth of the labor parties, the general hostility between squatter and swagman. He would not need to mull this over; awareness of it would be part of his response to 'Waltzing Matilda'.

It is now possible to suggest what may have been at least one of the reasons why 'Waltzing Matilda' did not become a national rallying song during the First World War; the soldiers of 1914-1918 were too close to the troubles of the Nineties; they or their fathers had often taken an active part on one side or the other. But by the Second World War the situation was different. The troubles of the Nineties had not been forgotten, but they had been healed. The soldier of 1939 could look back on the strikes with satisfaction, for they had in the final result contributed to the good life Australians enjoy. In 1895 the song must have seemed a plea that the spirit of the swagman should not be allowed to perish; in 1939 it would be seen as an affirmation that the spirit of the swagman had survived.

There is no information in the Mitchell Library file about William Power and that the author chanced upon this article long after research concerning the Shearers' Strikes of the Nineties had been completed. It came as a complete surprise to find that another party had written of a link between these strikes and Waltzing Matilda.

Before we leave the subject of the strikes, it is interesting to know that A.B. Paterson came very close to standing for Parliament. The first occasion was in the year of the first great Shearers' Strike, 1891. This is recorded in a newspaper cutting in the Mitchell Library dated 13th June of that year:

Arthur Barton Paterson, solicitor, one of the most cultured of young Australians, will stand for Yass Plains in the democratic interest. He is identical with no less a personage than the horsey-poet 'Banjo' whose 'Old Pardon, the Son of Reprieve' and 'Clancy of the Overflow' are known to all men. 'The Bulletin' hopes to have the pleasure of welcoming to the new parliament so bright and downright a son of the soil!

In 1942, Matilda crept into an English

'An affirmation that the spirit of the swagman had survived.'

The Opening Ceremony at the Twelfth Commonwealth Games, Brisbane, 1982.

periodical called *Poetry for the People*. It was introduced thus: *It was "Banjo" Paterson, the petit bourgeois, who wrote the words, the classic song of the class war in the pastoral phase of Australian history.*

It was interesting to note that both *The Star Spangled Banner* and *John Brown's Body*, although Oscar Mendelsohn cited them by way of contrast to our song, do have features remarkably like those of Matilda. Both the United States and Australia have plenty of heroic deeds in their histories worthy of commemoration without picking these silly episodes! Compare too the mad John Brown with our suicidal swagman.

On page ten of his book, Mendelsohn argues that rallying songs all must have one essential quality — ferocity. Surely the apprehension of one lonely swagman by three policemen and a squatter, with the swagman's sudden suicide, is enough ferocity for *Waltzing Matilda* to qualify?

The reader may take plenty of time to answer the questions posed in this case which has been put by a bushman from the Matilda country to solve a riddle constructed and confused by Southern academics. There is no hurry, because *Waltzing Matilda* will be around for a long time. However, many of the facts presented in this book could not now be found, because many of the people who provided them have passed into the silence since this research was done.

It is to those pioneers and their many unsung contemporary heroes of the tough but romantic Australian bush that this work is dedicated. It is they who deserve the credit for solving the long riddle that was the story of our song's genesis. Nobody but a bushman with the help of bush people could have solved that riddle. Many city people also gave enthusiastic assistance. It was in the capital cities too where many retired bush people added vital pieces of evidence. One of these was A. B. Paterson's son, Hugh. He was delighted to say during a conversation, "I am almost certain that my father wrote about the burning of Dagworth woolshed in one of his books. I shall make a search for it, because, if it is there, it will prove that you are on the right track." Hugh was really thrilled when he was able to say that his father had written of the episode in *Three Elephant Power and Other Stories*.

It is to all of those who helped and particularly those of the Winton-Kynuna district who started it all off that the following compliment is due. It

Evening at the Combo billabong, Diamantina River, Queensland.

comes in a resumé of all previous books about the song by Graham Jenkin in his text for *Pro Hart's Waltzing Matilda*, (Rigby, 1979):

The events leading up to the writing of 'Waltzing Matilda' are so interesting and have created so much controversy that a number of books and countless articles have been written about them. In fact it would be most surprising if there exists another single song about which so much has been written. In 1973, however, Richard Magoffin published the book which will almost certainly remain the definitive study, simply because, by dint of painstaking research, he has proven, once and for all, that the generally held belief regarding the song was quite correct. In addition, Magoffin has revealed a number of other aspects and details which not only support the accepted account, but provide further fascination to an already very interesting story. Other researchers such as Sydney May, who wrote the first book on 'Matilda' in 1944, and Harry Pearce, whose work appeared in 1971, also contributed substantially to our knowledge of the evolution of this remarkable song. Even the least reputable book on 'Matilda' — that by Oscar Mendelsohn — has played its part in piecing the story together. It so annoyed Magoffin by its incredible assertions that it moved him to pursue his own research with even greater energy and thoroughness. The following account draws material from various sources, but acknowledges by far its greatest debt to Richard Magoffin's excellent book: Fair Dinkum Matilda.

The search began, as the song did, at Dagworth, Kynuna, and Winton and, in the end, all trails led back to the song's home country.

From the upper Diamantina by a thousand channels, by the flickering flames of a thousand campfires when this land was young, the bushmen sang this haunting song and its people into history. Wherever the bush called them, its people answered and went, wherever cattle grazed or sheep were shorn. From the Diamantina and the Western River, to the Flinders, to the Paroo, the Darling and the Roper:

Hurrah for the Roma railway! Hurrah for Cobb and Co.,
And oh! for a good fat horse or two to carry me Westward Ho —
To carry me Westward Ho! my boys, that's where the cattle stray
On the far Barcoo, where they eat Nardoo, a thousand miles away.'
Then give your horses rein across the open plain,
We'll ship our meat both sound and sweet, nor care what some folks say;
And frozen we'll send home the cattle that now roam
On the far Barcoo and the Flinders too, a thousand miles away.

Wherever men worked stock, as they drifted with the dust of the muster, the songs of the bush went with them across the continent.

Now, these men are gone and their mustering camps, their wayside pubs, and most of their songs and stories, have gone with them.

Waltzing Matilda remains, partly because of its music, but more than anything, because of the story it tells. That story began three quarters of a century ago when Bob Macpherson told it to Banjo Paterson on the shady banks of the Combo billabong. It will never die.

The swagman died, but his ghost lives on, calling us to remember the pioneers, including those who came in chains to this harsh land. He calls us to remember the weak, the poor and the unemployed in our prosperous society. The ghost calls to authorities too, warning them to remember that the rights of the individual are paramount in our democratic way of life.

The ghost of that long dead swagman lives on to waltz along with his faithful travelling companion, Matilda. Long live Matilda — song of Australia. May she live as long as Australians are prepared to say, *Fair go, mate!*

'And his ghost may be heard as it sings in the billabong, 'Who'll come a-waltzing Matilda with me?'

Appendix

A. "I am a constable of police at present on duty at Dagworth. I remember Saturday last. I arrived here that day and went on duty about 10.30 that night in company with the last witness watching the shed and adjoining huts. I was armed with a carbine and revolver and 59 rounds of ammunition. I was to remain on duty till 2.30 the following morning.
About half past 12 I heard a volley of shots fired from the downs side about 50 yards from the shed.
I was about 10 or 15 yards from the corner of the shed between it and the huts.
I heard one shot strike the iron of a hut and several whistled past me.
I fired in the direction of the flashes (3 shots). The attacking party returned the fire and one of the attacking party called out from I should say about 40 yards 'Put up your arms you bastards or die.'
I went to a heap of earth close to the shed for cover and from there fired 3 or 4 shots in the direction of the attacking party. I then came to the nearest hut occupied by Messrs. Macpherson brothers and Mr Dyer to advise them of the position of affairs. I was joined by Mr Dyer and returned to the heap of earth. He was armed with a Winchester rifle.
We fired 7 or 8 shots each and then saw a match struck at the shed immediately followed by a blaze as if from kerosene. We both fired in the direction of the match. After some time the fire reached the roof of the shed, all this time the attacking party kept up a continuous fire under which it was impossible to reach the shed.
I heard the same voice say before the match was struck 'Give it to the bastards. We have waited long enough for this and now we'll have it.'
When we fired on the place where the match was struck the same voice sang out:— 'Rally up there chaps.' The voice appeared to be within thirty yards from the shed and about forty yards from where we were, the attacking party still continued the firing. The shed was completely burnt except one corner. I could see none of the atacking party; it was a very dark night. When the shed blazed up the attacking party retired further back.
I could not recognize the voice again. I don't know if I wounded any of the attacking party.
At daylight I examined the ground from where the attacking party was firing and found four discharged cartridges and two loaded ones, some were within 20 yards of the shed.
I occupied that night, when not on watch, the hut nearest the shed.
The next morning I found three bullet holes in it. One passed through the wall at the head of the bunk I occupy and lodged in the inner door.
If I had been in that bunk when the shot was fired I must have been shot. I also saw fresh bullet marks in the walls of the other huts one of which was occupied by a woman and two children.
It rained the morning after the fire sufficient to obliterate all tracks.
I was present when the police examined the body of a man named Hoffmeister 15 miles from here Sunday last. He had a Martini sporting rifle with him and 68 rounds of ammunition for it. The rifle appeared to be recently used. He also had 29 exploded rifle cartridges, a revolver and 21 cartridges. I found a similar exploded cartridge case at the place where the men were firing on the shed. There might have been others I did not find. I found a bullet in the hut I occupied and also found one in one of the other huts.
A search was made for the tracks of the attacking party but without success. It was quite impossible from where I was firing for me to fire the shots into the huts which were partly in my rear. The bullets entered from the opposite side from where I was. The huts fired on were quite out of the line of fire of the attacking party when firing on the shed. The fire on the huts could not be accidental.
Hoffmeister was a unionist shearer and had his union tickets on his body which was found in a unionist camp."
M. Daly

B. 'I am manager of Dagworth Station. I was to have commenced shearing on 15th August but no men signed. I intended afterwards to start shearing with a few men this week.
I was at the woolshed on the night of 1st inst. and had about 20 men. I have had the shed watched for about 5 weeks to protect it from being burnt by unionists. I was aroused about midnight of the 1st by a volley of shots. I was in the hut nearest the shed, got up and procured a revolver from my brother after some time. Before that I heard a voice call out 'Hold up your hands or die' and afterwards. 'Hold up your hands you bastards or die.'
Dyer went away with Constable Daly and when I got a revolver I followed.
When I saw a flash of 3 or 4 shots about 40 yards away from the attacking party, I returned the fire and immediately heard a bullet whistle past me. I fired five more shots — the attacking party kept up a continuous fire.
I could see Dyer, Daly and Tomlin returning the fire.

Before the shed was set fire to I heard the same voice say: 'Rally up boys and let them have it. You'll die or we'll die." I saw the shed on fire. It was impossible to attempt to save it in consequence of the incessant firing of the attacking party.

About 140 lambs and other property were burnt in the shed. The firing continued on and off for ¾ of an hour and only ceased when the shed was fully at large.

I attempted to save the lambs and some wool but was fired on by the attacking party and retired. It was too dark for me to see any of the men.

I think I recognized the voice and could identify it again. The shed was completely burnt all but a small corner.

I examined the place at daylight and saw several empty and full cartridges picked up from 10 to 30 yards from the shed, 26 were found.

I saw melted bullets in the shed, and one taken out of an inner door in the hut nearest the shed — 3 bullets were fired at that hut.

If one man had been in his bunk, he would have been shot. In another hut fired at there were 14 men. In another hut fired at there was a woman and her two daughters.

Neither I nor the other defenders could have fired the shots at the huts.

The attacking party firing at the shed and its defenders could not have accidentally hit any of the huts especially the one containing the woman which was about 200 yards off the line of fire.

From the words used I think the attacking party were unionists. The words then used are commonly used by unionists. It was very dark. I could not see any there nor do I know of any being wounded.

It rained before daylight sufficient to destroy all tracks which I searched for without success.

The cartridge cases picked up were principally Winchester rifle and some Martini Henry and some revolver.

It was known I intended to shear this week uner '94 agreement.

The woolshed is six miles from the main road.

I found three gates open near the shed, one leading to the head-station and two towards the back country.

R.R.Macpherson'

C. From the telegram sent by Eglinton the following day, it is obvious that he connects the Hoffmeister suicide with the foray at the shed:
From Ayrshire Dns.
8.50 a.m.
The Hon Secretary
Brisbane (10.00 a.m.)
'Held enquiry at Dagworth woolshed re burning. Unionists at the time they fired on the defenders of the shed also fired on a hut quite out of line of the shed. One of the huts containing the wife and daughters of a man known to be unfriendly to unionists. None of the unionists identified — Hoffmeister suicided fourteen miles from Dagworth woolshed morning after the fire and had a rifle and a large number of loaded and exploded cartridges corresponding with some exploded cartridges found at place from where unionists fired on shed.

D. 'I am a shearer and bush man at present residing at the Shearers' Camp, Kynuna. I have been there about a week — I arrived there last Sunday week from Richmond by Maxwelton and Hamilton Downs, with William Gumley. I shifted from the Shearers' Camp the early part of last week and camped down the Dagworth Road about 4 miles away — Gumley was the only one with me.

I am on strike. I left the Camp on the road for Winton. I left the Camp at before dinner or shortly after — I was waiting there for the mail — five or six men joined my camp. There was Edward Dempsey, Chris Connolly and his mate Named Bob, one Moody and his mate Bill who were there before, Jack Crimmins and his mate Jim, the deceased, who was known as 'Frenchy' and a foot man whose name I do not know. Crimmins and his mate came in Friday night and the deceased on Saturday evening, I don't know where they came from. I did not see any of them when I was camped in the Union Camp at Kynuna. They never told me where they came from — they were all horsemen bar one who is here.

When Frenchy came it looked like rain, he came about sundown. He appeared sober. I heard his voice but did not hear what he said. He came from the direction of the Kynuna Camp.

I had a tent pitched. Frenchy did not pitch anything. Frenchy was mounted and leading a packhorse. He slept beneath a tree between me and another fly.

I went to bed about 8 or 9. It was before 10. No one occupied my tent but myself some of the others had gone to bed before me. I saw them all in bed that night about 2.

They might have been absent when I was asleep. I did not speak to anyone when I got out. It had not rained when I went out. I went to bed again and woke at dawn. It was raining.

Frenchy rolled up his swag and put it in my tent and went to the fire and afterwards was walking about in the camp by himself. There were several at the fire, of these I have mentioned.

I remained lying down in the tent. There were no horses about the Camp while it was raining. There could not be any horses without my knowing it at dawn, about the Camp.

All the men were in the Camp in the morning and remained there in the forenoon including Frenchy who was walking up and down the Camp. He did not speak to me. We had dinner between 12 and 1. Frenchy had his dinner at the fire, others were there, no strangers.

After dinner Frenchy came to the fire and I saw him burning some papers and heard him mutter something like 'That done I am satisfied'. He walked away about twenty yards — I heard a report of firearms and went in that direction and saw Frenchy lying down partly on his left side near a fly occupied by Crimmins and his mate. I did not notice if anything was on it — some of my mates were at the body before I got there. They were looking on. I thought he was dead. There was a revolver pouch near his back and a revolver about his chest somewhere

— I saw blood about his mouth. I went away, got my horses and reported it to Mr McCowan.

The first time I saw the revolver was when it was close to his body. I did not touch it or see anyone else do so.

After seeing Mr McCowan, I returned to the camp and covered up the body and left the camp the same evening and went to the Kynuna Union Camp.

As Frenchy was not walking, I assumed he was a unionist. I was friendly towards him, so were the others.

There was no quarrel or dispute between Frenchy and myself or any other man that I know of — I assume that he shot himself, but why I can't say.

On the night it rained (Saturday night) no one called at the camp.

I did not come down Workingham Creek from Sesbania.

It was a revolver and pouch like the one produced that I saw with Frenchy when he put his swag in my tent. He also put in a rifle too.

I don't know of any other rifles in the camp but Frenchy's.

He appeared to me to be in good health on Sunday morning. He had a good turnout.

I am a single man and have no settled place of abode.

Neil Highland
Taken and Sworn before me at Kynuna
this fifth day of September 1894.
Ernest Eglinton, PM.'

The evidence of the other witnesses is summarised here for comparison:

William Moody:
The men selected their camp because the grass was better there than at Kynuna. Hoffmeister camped the night in Highland's tent. Moody twice stated that Highland had lied. Hoffmeister burnt an envelope with postmarks. The deceased was said to be 'a bit barmy'.

Lewis Murray:
He had come from Brisbane and had been in the area for five weeks. He saw 'the police **going down**'. Hoffmeister had the only rifle in the camp.

Senior Constable Austin Cafferty:
He was stationed at Kynuna. He was advised of the death by Mr McCowan of Kynuna Station. He found fresh blood coming from the dead man's mouth. Highland told him the revolver was Hoffmeister's.

William Goode:
The revolver was his and Moody (his mate) was present when he fired it last. He heard some of the men say Frenchy was 'a bit mad'.

E. "I hereby certify that on the twenty-ninth day of September, 1891, I held an Inquest of Death at Dagworth Station in the Police District of Winton and that the following particulars were then disclosed:-

Name of deceased:	George Hamlyn Pope
Profession or calling:	Woolscourer
Height, colour of hair, peculiar clothing, and any other means of identity:	Height about 5 ft 6 ins Colour of hair — dark brown
Where found and when:	In Scour Waterhole at Dagworth Station on Seventeenth September, 1891.
Date of death:	Sixteenth or seventeenth September. 1891.
Supposed cause of death:	Drowning
Persons last seen in company of deceased, and names of suspected persons:	_____
Accused:	_____
Names, residences and callings of witnesses:	Jacob Woods, scour overseer, Dagworth Stn. Thomas Richardson, scour hand, Dagworth Stn. Benjamin Brett, wool roller, Dagworth Stn.
Suspicious circumstances:	None

R.R.Macpherson
Justice.

The enquiry was dated 24th November, 1891 by the Justice Department and numbered 432.

F. 'I must impress upon you that I was very young when we lived at Kynuna. My earliest recollection of the song was in 1897. My father — Adam Black — took over the management of Kynuna on 17th March that year. The Macpherson Bros. were at Dagworth and gave my mother one of the original copies of the verses, written on notepaper. They told of the happy party of which Banjo Paterson was a guest and his so recently composed song such a success — and also at Mrs. Riley's home in Winton where it was a great hit.

The first and only tune I know for 'Waltzing Matilda' is the one first heard at Kynuna. The newer words and tune do not appeal to me so have never bothered to learn them. I always understood the tune was an old Scottish or Irish one.

Yes, I think 'Waltzing Matilda' is a song of social significance and should be preserved in its original way. Pleased to help you in your endeavour to save 'Waltzing Matilda' from being spoilt by new words and tunes, also pleased if you would visit us some time.

I am interested in the long controversy about the song and think it should be left as we have known and loved it all these years. Other countries have folksongs handed down for generations. Why can't Queensland have 'Waltzing Matilda' left as it is and not spoilt by 'Pop' or 'Jazz'?

Re Mr May's book — Mother had an autographed copy but I cannot find it. In 'Banjo of the Bush' (page 91) the top line in each verse is exactly the same as we learnt it and sang to the tune we have known all these years. It was impressed on me that Banjo Paterson wrote the words at Dagworth.

I know nothing of the Cloncurry version.

My parents often spoke of the 'shearers strike' and I think they were then at Eldersleigh (where I was born) or at Ayrshire Downs. They spoke of the arrival of mounted men, sent to try and protect property etc. We had left the district before Dagworth shed was burnt or the shearer shot.

I'm sure Robert Macpherson found the swaggie with the dead sheep but not sure if a policeman ever arrived on the scene. As a child I liked to think he did!

Wishing you success on Matilda's behalf,

Yours sincerely,
Violet Allingham'

G. Much has been written about what Paterson did or did not say about the song. However, it is quite ridiculous and stupid to pretend that he did not claim the work as his own very clearly. Apart from publishing 'Waltzing Matilda' as his own in 1917 and from then on, he has several statements on record.

One authentically documented statement was purposefully recorded not long before Paterson died, by his old journalist colleague, Vince Kelly, in an article for 'The Sun'. The poet's exact words to Kelly were:

'It was such a catchy, provocative, whimsical tune that I said to her, 'Why don't you sing the words to that?'

She replied, 'It hasn't got any words that I know of, but it must have had at one time. I believe it was an old Scottish hymn.'

It was then that I decided it should have words to keep it alive — I wrote words which I thought expressed its whimsicality and dreaminess.'

(The foregoing statement is taken from an undated newspaper cutting included in the files of the late Sydney May. The cutting is a review by Vince Kelly himself of John Manifold's 'Who wrote the Ballads' published in 1964).

H. It is most interesting to compare the foregoing statement with one written by Paterson in the from of a letter to Mr Laurie Copping of Hall, Canberra. Mr Copping still has this letter which was dated June 16th, 1939. It reads:

'I wrote it when travelling in Queensland.

A Miss Macpherson, afterwards Mrs McCowan, used to play a tune which she believed was an old Scottish tune, but she did not know the name of it.

I put words to it.

I am sorry to say I do not know if it is included in any of my books. My wife says it is not.

It may interest your literary circle to know that the tune is played in the continent of Europe as it is supposed to be the only existing Australian folk song.

I have had enquiries from them as to the origin of the tune, but the lady who played it did not know who wrote it.'

I. An excerpt from Paterson's "Three Elephant Power and Other Stories", p. 100. This shows his intimate knowledge of events at Dagworth woolshed, just prior to his visit.

"Dogs, like horses, have very keen intuition. They know when the men around them are frightened, though they may not know the cause. In a great Queensland strike, when the shearers attacked and burnt Dagworth shed, some rifle-volleys were exchanged. The air was full of human electricity, each man giving out waves of fear and excitement. Mark now the effect it had on the dogs. They were not in the fighting; nobody fired at them, and nobody spoke to them; but every dog left his master, left the sheep, and went away to the homestead, about six miles off. There wasn't a dog about the shed next day after the fight. The noise of the rifles had not frightened them, because they were well-accustomed to that."

AUTHOR'S NOTE

Paterson's personal papers and diaries have recently been researched by his grand-daughters for publication of his 'Complete Works'. The diary makes reference to his writing of 'Waltzing Matilda' at Dagworth and the papers include a hand-written manuscript of the song's words with corrections, as well as a clean copy. It has not been possible to present that material in this history, because publication is necessarily restricted until release of the above work. However, the family is conversant with the author's work and have assured him that there is nothing in the new material which conflicts with his basic account of events.

WALTZING MATILDA
Original 1895 Macpherson Version, arranged by
R. Magoffin and E. Berryman for The Towers
Players. Copyright 1982.

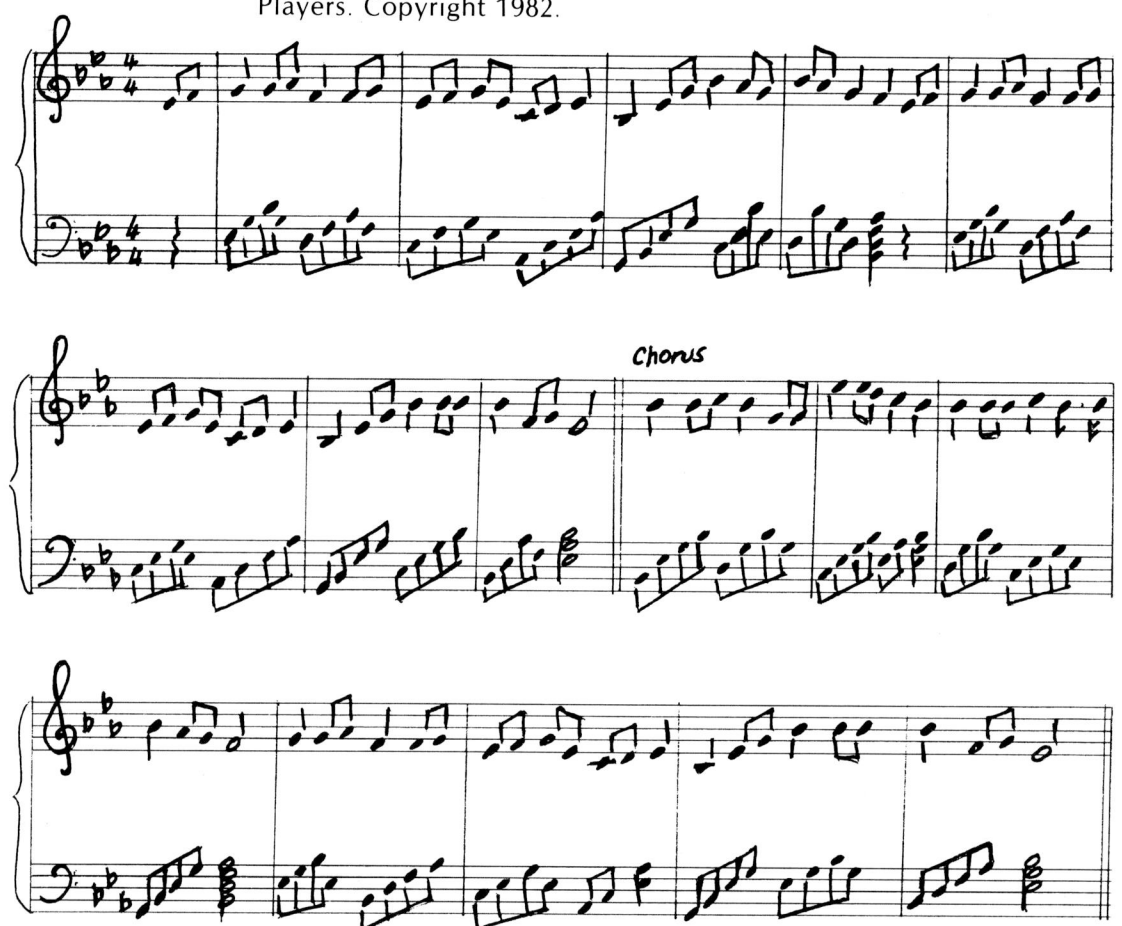

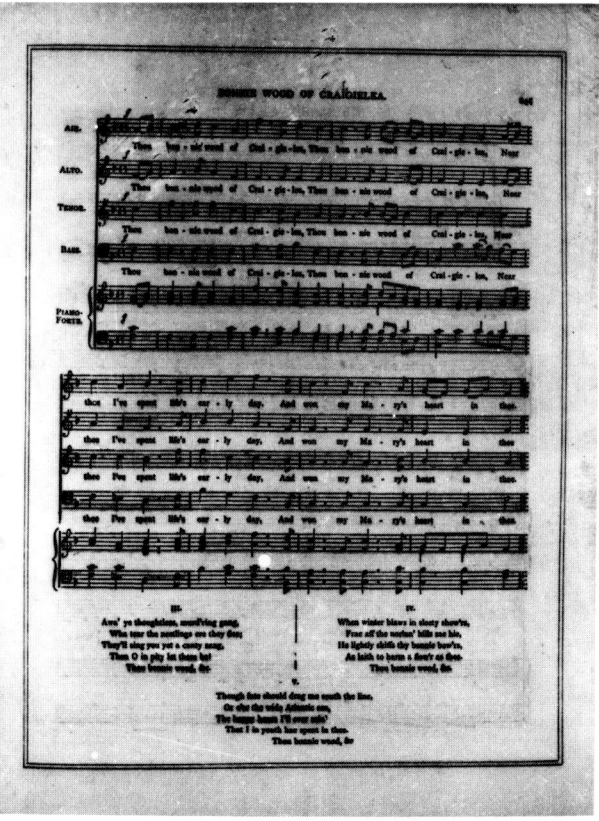

Christina Macpherson, composer

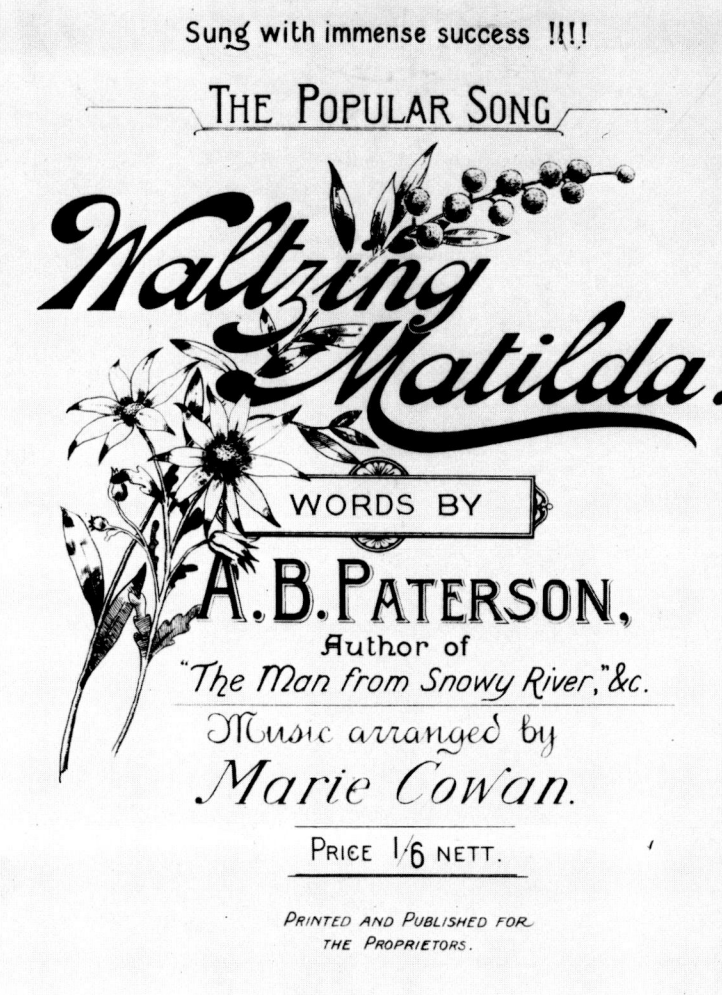

James Inglis and Co. publication, 1903, Sydney

Bob Macpherson, squatter

Andrew Barton Paterson, poet

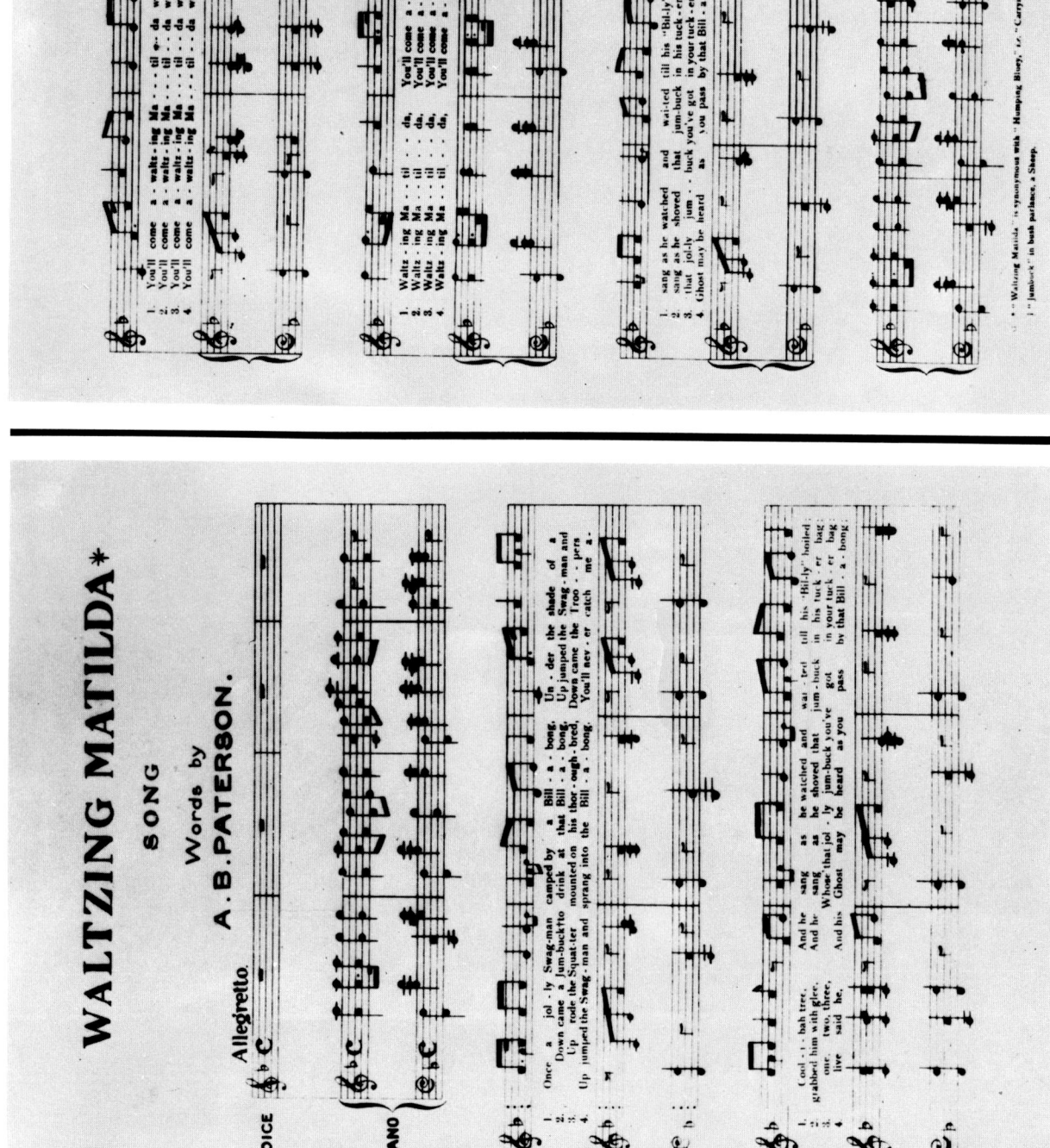

James Inglis and Company's publication of 'Waltzing Matilda', printed to advertise their 'Billy Tea', 1903. Marie Cowan is clearly shown to be arranger only. She altered the tune. Paterson's words were altered for advertising purposes and the swagman became 'jolly' waiting for his billy to boil.

Mrs Marie Riley, at whose home, *Aloha*, in Vindex Street, Winton, the song was first played on a piano and the music committed to paper.

A.B. Paterson was engaged to Mr Riley's sister, Sarah, when he visited Winton. Sarah was a schoolfriend of Christina Macpherson.

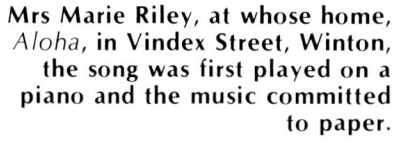

Vindex Street

'Aloha'

Frederick Whistler Riley, his wife, Marie, and a stable-hand.

Jane Black, who, with her husband, Adam, had an early association with the song, Kynuna, 1897.

John Tait Wilson, book-keeper at Dagworth. He was away on leave when the song was written, but it was on his auto-harp that Christina played the tune which became 'Waltzing Matilda'.

Walter J. Roebuck, telegraph operator, and Jack Carter, overseer. Roebuck held an early copy of the song. Carter used the expression 'Waltzing Matilda' at dinner, one night.

Winton district identities in the Nineties. Bob Macpherson — third from the left, centre row.

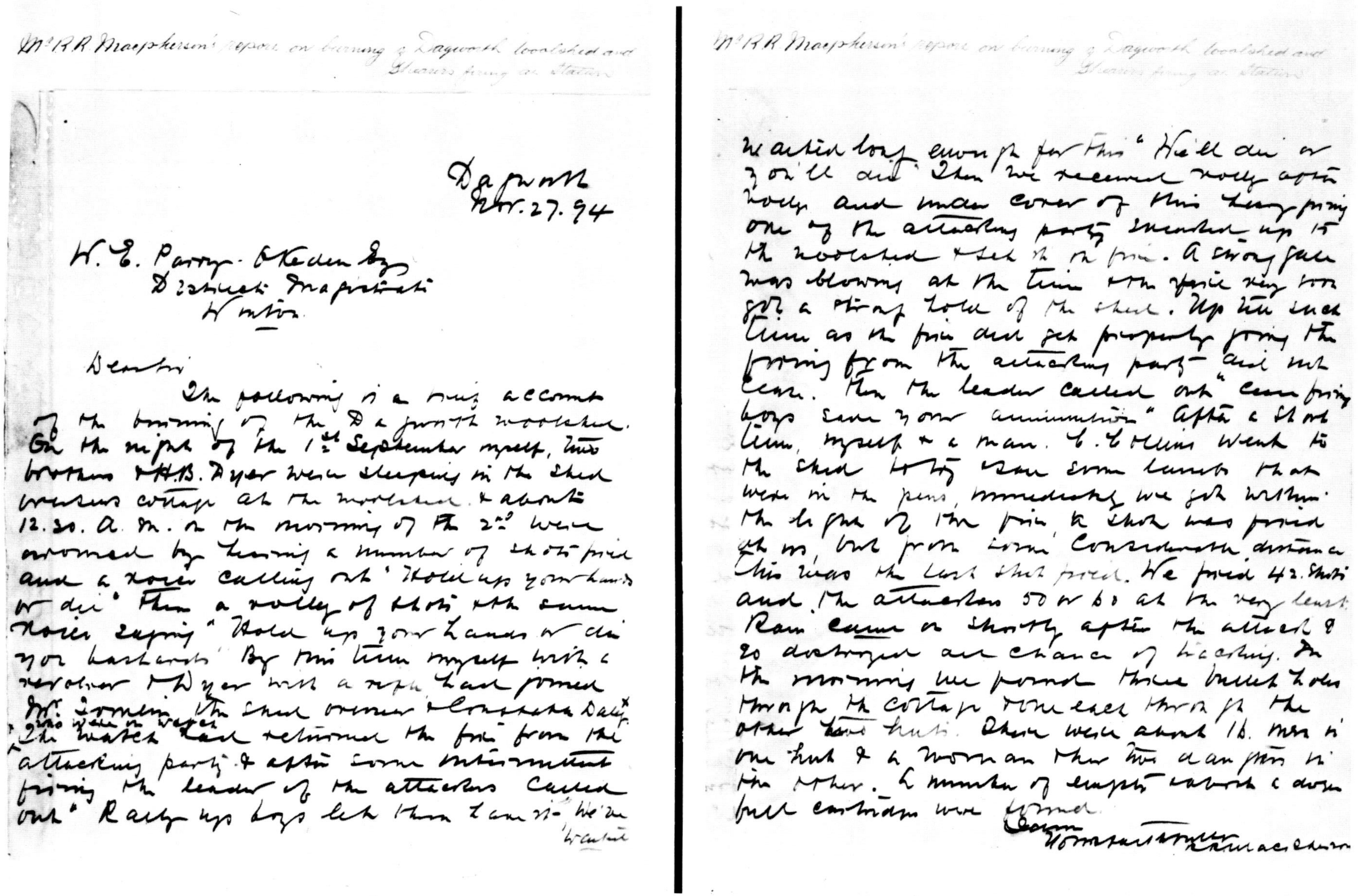

Dagworth
Sept 27. 94

W. E. Parry-Okeden Esq.
District Magistrate
Winton

Dear Sir

The following is a brief account of the burning of the D. & Dagworth woolshed. On the night of the 1st September myself, two brothers W.P.S. & H.B. Dyer were sleeping in the shed overseer's cottage at the woolshed & about 12.30 a.m. on the morning of the 2nd were aroused by hearing a number of shots fired and a voice calling out "Hold up your hands or die" then a volley of shots with same voice saying "Hold up your hands or die you bastards." By this time myself W.P. & my brother H.B. had got hold of our rifles & revolvers & returned the fire from the cottage & after some minutes' firing the leader of the attackers called out "Rally up boys let us then 2 run 2 — hit on retreat"

& a similar long event to that "He'll never do it out." Then we seemed really after some of the attacking party however up to the woolshed where a big fire was blazing at the time & we saw fire . a short period . as he didn't know the voice. We the [over?] time as we fired our gun property and we could see from the attacking party "All but one." Then the leader called out "come boys run you ammunition." After I did not limit myself to a man. W.P. Mc went to the shed but by this time their [?] were in no position movement we got within 30 yds . of the fire & the fire was over within 3 m of the [?] fire to Corrimpon's moving. This was the [last?] that passed. He fired 4 or 5 shots and the attackers 50 or 60 as they very [best?] . Ran even a chance of being hit or attacked. So everyone was clear of hearing. In the morning we found there were 9 men that we certain murderers there & the said bush. There were about 18. Men & the 2nd & 4 women & the two or an [?] to the upper. I thought their wounds were bad enough mm Guine

[signature]

Macpherson Brothers at Dagworth in the Nineties. Sitting (l to r): Angus Macpherson, Bob Macpherson, Edward Blurton. Standing: Jack and Gideon Macpherson.

Kynuna identities
Standing: Walter Roebuck and Bob Macpherson. Sitting (l to r): Jack Kay, Mick Fahey, and Richard Magoffin, the author's grandfather.

Winton scenes from an 1897 calendar

About the Author

Born at Cloncurry in 1937, Richard Magoffin has spent all his life between that outback town and his present home in the historic gold town, Charters Towers. He managed family sheep properties during the difficult Sixties, until droughts and low wool prices forced him, with many others, to take another track.

This was an experience shared with the squatter of *Waltzing Matilda*. Bob Macpherson left Dagworth Station in 1906 after a series of droughts with only his swag and a buckboard. He returned to the district in his later years and the author's grandfather was present, with other friends, when Bob collapsed and died at the Kynuna Hotel, in July, 1930. He was buried at Dagworth beside his brother, Jack, who was overseer when Banjo Paterson wrote *Waltzing Matilda* at the station homestead in January, 1895.

Richard Magoffin lived only 35 kms away at Quambetook Station, which adjoined Dagworth in the early days. So, he grew up with the Matilda legend.

Several books about the song by southern writers had it all wrong, so, in 1968, Magoffin set about turning a local legend into national history. Many of those who provided him with first hand evidence have since died. Had the author not commenced his long search when he did, the riddle that was the story of Australia's best known song would not have been solved.

Earlier books have earned Magoffin wide acclaim as a bush balladist in the genre of Paterson, Lawson, Ogilvie and John O'Brien. So, he shares with Paterson the insight of a poet. This insight, with his local knowledge of people, places, and events associated with the song, permeates this folk-history, so that the reader can almost scent the eucalyptus of coolibahs on the Diamantina River. This is a feature of all Richard Magoffin's books, which have delighted thousands of Australians, city-dwellers and bushies alike.